How To
Day Trade
Stocks
For Profit

Harvey Walsh

First Published 2004
Fourth Edition Published 2015
[P4.00]

Shelfless Ltd
1 Church Hill
Leigh-on-Sea SS9 2DE
United Kingdom
www.shelfless.co.uk

PRAISE FOR HOW TO DAY TRADE STOCKS FOR PROFIT

"This is by far the best course I've ever read. I paid over $5,000 for seven days of school for day trading. It does not even come close to what you are teaching."
- *Donnell Smith*

"...have been using the info in your book for three days. $1,490 in the bank...The best thing about the book is that it not only tells you what to do, but why you should do it."
- *John Foy*

"I've worked in the world of training for almost 20 years and I have to say I have found your training manual to be one of the most comprehensive and straight forward that I have ever read. Started trading this week using your strategies on the FTSE and my account is up 25%."
- *David Mac*

"...very inexpensive for a straight-to-the-point trading course that actually works!"
- *Leo Tognetti*

"Yesterday I made an average of 46 cents per/share [$460] for 3 trades, the previous day I did 36 cents/share [$360]"
- *Chris Verm*

"...such a great trading course. For the money [$197 at the time], it is easily the best course on the market."
- *John Coan*

"I've been paper trading for the last four days and have an average gain of 1.25 points per day [$1,250] with no losses (I'm pretty proud of it actually)."
- *Rob in Toronto*

"..after several months of practicing your day trading principles outlined in your book, I ended my first day of live trading with a net profit of $279.53"
- *Peter Scott*

"I've now made about 350% in 4 months and am close to earning the equivalent of my annual wage and can see a way to break free from my day job."
- *Michael Snoswell*

"It was a great day! I made a $1,175.50 profit...I was real happy with the results, but I wanted to make sure it wasn't a fluke or something, but I had to wait until Monday...the day felt slow in comparison to Friday, I made a couple of hundred dollars."
- *Salvador Alba*

"..simply superb. Excellent material"
- *Jeffrey Powell*

"You are an amazing trader and a very gifted teacher. I diligently studied your book. You opened my eyes to a whole new world of possibilities."
- *Micah Brunson*

"...ever since I have studied your system I have improved so much as a trader and have grown my account very nicely...I am already making my job salary in trading."
- *Jaime Leal*

Risk Disclosure Statement

Day trading has large potential rewards, and also large potential risk. You must be aware of the risks and be willing to accept them in order to invest in the stock markets. Do not trade with money that you cannot afford to lose. The contents of this book is for general information purposes only. Although every attempt has been made to assure accuracy, we assume no responsibility for errors or omissions. Examples are provided for illustrative purposes and should not be construed as investment advice or strategy. Hypothetical or simulated performance results have certain inherent limitations; unlike an actual performance record, simulated results do not represent actual trading. Also, since the trades have not actually been executed, the results may have under or over compensated for the impact, if any, of certain market factors, such as lack of liquidity. Past performance is not indicative of future results.

CONTENTS

Introduction To The Third Edition

The first edition of this book was published more than ten years ago. Since then, much of the world has seen the largest recession in living memory. Even now, after the worst is apparently over, the news still seems to be full of downbeat stories of low inflation, low or negative growth, tumbling interest rates, poorly performing investments, and stagnating or falling wages. At the same time there are, we are told, more billionaires than ever. The rich are getting richer. The gap between the haves and have-nots has never been greater.

What is it that those who are making money know, that the rest of the world doesn't? Is it true that money leads to more money? That the only way to prosper in an economic downturn is have a fortune in the bank at the outset?

I don't think so. In fact, I know that's not the case. The truth is, there is always an abundance of opportunity, you just need to know where to look.

Some discover opportunities in salvaging great ideas or brilliant products from dying companies, giving them a new lease of life and taking them to new heights. Some find their fortunes by coming up with new ideas, innovative products or amazing services that the world just can't do without, even in hard times. These are all admirable ways to make a living, but it takes a certain kind of person to pull them off. The sort of person who works long and hard. The sort of person who never switches off. The sort of person I am most certainly not.

You see I am, I must admit, quite lazy. It's what got me into trading. The idea of "working" just a few hours a day has a certain appeal. You probably find it appealing too, which is why you're reading this book. Naturally, that sort of person wonders if all this negative news means that trading for a living is no longer viable. After all, if stock markets are falling, then there's no money to be made there, right?

Wrong. Without wishing to sound mercenary, bad news like good, is the life blood of the stock market. For every company having a terrible day, you can be sure there's another one somewhere that's having its best day ever. Stock traders can profit from both of them.

It doesn't matter how bad the economy gets, for those of us who know how to find them, there will always be amazing opportunities that we can *day trade for profit*. Every single day. The aim of this book is to teach you how to find those opportunities, and to trade them for the best return. Rest assured, however bad the news channels like to make out things have got, there are always great trades to be had.

This is the fourth major revision of *How To Day Trade Stocks For Profit*. Despite that, very little has actually changed since the first edition more than ten years ago. The trading strategy I present to you here is exactly the same as it was back then. The method works just as well now as it did then. If anything, it's better, because economic turmoil means there's even more movement in stock prices. Movement means opportunity, which means potential profit.

That said, there have been some updates. Some of the services I have recommended over the years have changed or disappeared altogether. Those have been replaced with alternatives, or newer, better recommendations. Many of the illustrations in this fourth edition have also been jazzed up, making them clearer and easier to read.

Fundamentally though, the core principles, and the strategy that is built upon them, are unchanged. All of which means that what you are holding in your hands is a way to make money that is proven to stand the test of time, whatever the future holds.

How To Use This Book

This is a work in four parts. Whilst it can be tempting to jump ahead and go straight for the good stuff, the nitty gritty on specific trading setups, I urge you to be patient and read through everything in order. Like building a new house, building a set of skills requires solid foundations. They may not be the most exciting part of the process, but without them everything can come crumbling down when it matters most.

So Part One of the book, *Trading Foundation*, lays down those all important underpinnings. Even if you've already done some trading, it is well worth reading Part One. I never cease to be amazed at how many 'traders' have somewhat confused ideas about the very basics of the subject. Part One will make sure you have a good solid understanding of how the markets work. This alone will put you ahead of 80% of other market participants, and as we shall see, any edge you can gain will ultimately help you become more profitable. Part One also deals with trading psychology (which is the hardest part of this business), as well as how to get set up and actually start trading

Part Two gives you a chance to test your newly built foundations. Once laid, we need to know they are solid. Any cracks could lead to costly failings down the line. I will present you with some stock charts accompanied by questions. If you find you can't answer them easily, do go back and re-read the relevant section in Part One. The brain abhors a vacuum, and so when presented with a question it cannot answer, and then shown the information required to provide the answer, it sucks up that information with such force that it will remain firmly in place. These questions are an essential tool in learning, and again, I urge you to resist the temptation to skip them.

In Part Three, *The Trading Strategy*, I will pull back the curtain and show you exactly how I make my money, and how you can do the same. You will build on your solid, tested foundations, a strong and proven structure. It's a structure that plays to the way the market works at a most fundamental level. Unlike short term trading methods that are whipped together in a hurry to take advantage of transient market conditions, our structure will work as long as the markets are open and are traded by people. It will provide you with dependable, solid, profit generating trades every day for as long as you want to trade.

Finally, Part Four follows up with more questions and answers. Again, this will really help you consolidate everything you have read. Feedback from customers of the first two editions of this book have shown time and again that students who take it seriously, read everything, and take action and do the exercises, do better in their trading than those who simply skim the material looking for a few nuggets of information.

PART ONE - TRADING FOUNDATION

Chapter 1 - Trading Objectives

"If no one ever took risks, Michelangelo would have painted the Sistine floor"
Neil Simon

Why Trade?

The reasons people take up trading are varied, but there are two which account for the majority. The desire to make large amounts of money, and the desire for freedom from a traditional job.

For me, it was the freedom. I'd had enough of working for 'the man'. Not only did my efforts in the workplace go largely unnoticed, I saw they were making other people (the owners of the company) wealthy. The harder I worked, the richer they got. And the less enjoyable my life became. I saw less of my family, and more of a dull office. Something had to change.

Trading for a living gave me the freedom to work for just a few hours day. I could work from anywhere in the world with an internet connection. Take vacations whenever I felt like it. Spend quality time with my family. See my kids grow up. And certainly, the fact it put more cash into my bank account than my old day job ever could have hoped to have done didn't hurt!

Perhaps you've had similar thoughts, which is what has led you to this book. Or perhaps you want to trade to supplement the income from your job. Whatever your own personal reasons might be, I think you'll find making money from the markets fun and rewarding, and not just in the financial sense. So let's dive in, and learn *How To Day Trade Stocks For Profit*.

Defining Our Objective

Before we commence our journey, it is important to be clear about our destination. A simple statement of our ultimate goal will help us to keep focused: *"Our objective as day traders is to take consistent daily profits from the stock market."*

In other words we want to be able to make money every day. Does that sound like a reasonable goal? Great! Let's get building that foundation.

Why Day Trade Instead of Buy And Hold?

Traditional stock market investing is based on the process of buying stock in a company, holding it while the price — hopefully — goes higher, and then selling it for a profit. This is often called a *buy and hold* strategy. Whilst that certainly offers good profit potential, day trading offers us a number of advantages.

Firstly, stocks make lots of moves during the day, and as we'll see, these individual moves can add up to more potential profit than the longer term price movements associated with regular buy and hold trading.

Not only that, but day trading involves no exposure to the market at times we are not actively trading. That means we as day traders are at less risk from news events which can range from company profit warnings through to terrorist attacks.

Last but by no means least, by taking profits at the end of each day, we are provided with a steady income stream. We get to meet the *daily profits* part of our objective.

Let's go back and consider the first point briefly. Take a look at this chart (don't worry if you don't fully understand it just yet).

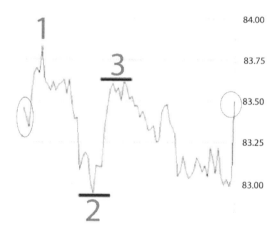

Using a buy and hold strategy we could have bought this stock — which happens to be IBM — at about $83.45 when the market opened (the first circle). At the end of the day it had risen to a closing price of $83.50, a gain of just $0.05 for every share we held.

As day traders, if we were able to buy at the lowest price during the day, which was about $82.90 (the point marked 2 on the chart), and sell about half an hour later at point 3, we would have realised a profit of $0.70 for every share, and not have any further exposure to the market. So not only would we have made substantially more money than if we had simply bought the stock and held on, we also wouldn't be worried if IBM suddenly issued a profits warning after the market closed, causing the price to fall, because we would no longer be holding any of its stock. More profit, less time in the market, and less stress. Sounds good, doesn't it?

How Do We Make Money From The Market?

In the simplest terms, we can make money in two ways:

1. We can buy stock at one price, and sell it at a higher price. When we buy stock to sell later on, we call this *going long*.

2. We can also sell stock we don't own, at one price, and buy it back at a lower price. When we sell stock we don't currently own with a view to buying it back later, we call this *going short*.

Going short, or short selling as it's also called, is a vital tool to us as day traders, because it means we can make money when prices are falling, not just when they're going up.

An example will make this clearer. Let's imagine we decide to sell 1000 shares in IBM at a price of $83.00 per share. We don't currently own any IBM stock, so our broker lends us some to sell. Once this stock is sold, our trading account is credited with the proceeds, i.e. $83,000 ($83 x 1000 shares). We are now *short* 1000 shares

At some point we have to buy back the stock so that we can give it back to our broker. If the price were to fall to $82.50 we may decide it's the right time to buy back our stock. This will cost us $82,500 ($82.50 x 1000 shares) thus leaving us with a profit of $500 ($83,000 credited from the sale - $82,500 spent to buy back the stock).

By the way, don't worry if buying and selling tens of thousands of dollars worth of stock sounds like it's out of your price range, later on I will show you how you can buy and sell using other people's money.

All this borrowing and paying back of stock might sound complicated and hard to keep track of, but in fact the process is entirely automatic and transparent, so we can go short and profit from falling prices just as easily as we can go long when we think prices will rise.

If you look back at the previous chart of the IBM stock, you can see that we could have gone short at point 1, and covered our position (bought back the shares we borrowed) at point 2, capturing a move of about $0.90 per share. Of course, we could then have gone long at point 2 and profited from the move back up to point 3, giving us a total profit of $1.60 per share in a period of just 2 hours, instead of the $0.05 per share had we held all day. All these moves happening through the day can add up to big money, and this is just one stock. When we consider there are thousands of stocks moving every day, it becomes apparent that the potential to make money from the stock market is gigantic.

So far so good, but there's an obvious question that presents itself at this point. How do we know whether the price of a stock is going to go up or down, and therefore whether we need to go long or short? The answer is we don't. We can only trade based on where we believe the greatest probability of the next price move lies.

Nobody can predict with 100% accuracy what direction a stock price is going to go in next, or how far in that direction it will go. However, we don't need 100% accuracy to make money. In fact, we don't even need 50% accuracy, as long as we manage each trade correctly.

Time for another example: Let's imagine we make ten trades on a particular day. On four of those trades, our predictions about which way the price will go are right and the trade is a winner (i.e. profitable). The six other trades don't go so well. In fact, our predictions for those six are completely wrong and we lose money on each of them. The average profit we got from from each of the four winning trades was $75.00. However, because we saw that the losing trades weren't going the way we hoped, we ended them quickly, making our average loss from each of them just $25.00. Our total profit from the four winning trades then, was $300.00 (4 winners x $75 per win). Our total loss from the six losing trades was $150.00 (6 losers x $25 per loss). Our net profit at the end of the day was $150.00 ($300 won - $150 lost).

So in this example, even though we were wrong about the market direction more times than we were right, we still made a profit. This was simply because we made sure that our losses were smaller than our profits. This brings us to Rule Number One of day trading, the importance of which cannot be overstated: End losing trades quickly, and let winning trades run as far as you can. This is something we must bear in mind as we go through the rest of this book. It is something that every trader knows they should do, but very few actually practice, and that is the most common difference between profitable traders, and losing ones.

Summary

Our job as day traders is to evaluate the probabilities of potential stock price movements, make trades by buying and selling stock based on those probabilities, and manage those trades effectively by minimising our loss when the market proves us wrong, and maximising our profit when we are right.

Clearly, a large part of our job is forming an opinion of future stock price direction based on probability. We can never know for sure what is going to happen next to any stock price, but the price itself does give us lots of clues as to what it is likely to do. We need to gather these clues and combine them to put us on the side of the greatest probability.

Now we need to look in some detail at how we find those clues, and form that initial opinion.

Ship via: Standard

QTY	Description	Loc	SKU/ISBN/UPC	Condition	Price
1	How To Day Trade Stocks For Profit [Paperback] [2013] Walsh, Harvey	[CKY40027373573@F-04-09-;1]	CKY40027373573 1484961749	Used; Good 100% Customer Satisfaction Guaranteed.	$12.12

Order# 127514426

(Amazon order #114-2136526-3536263)

Date ordered: 2015-09-21 13:28:53

We hope you enjoy your order!

From:

www.ckybooks.com
500 John C. Watts Drive
Suite B
Nicholasville,   KY   40356

ADRIAN A ALDAZ
3589 COCONUT WAY

OCEANSIDE CA 92058 United States

zpnxnb8scrx81s7@marketplace.amazon.com
Adrian Aldaz

CHAPTER 2 - ANALYSIS BASICS

"Buy land. They're not making it any more."
Mark Twain

Analysis Methods

We analyse the stock we are trading in order to form an opinion of where its price is likely to move next. There are two basic types of analysis traders can use:

- Fundamental Analysis (FA)
- Technical Analysis (TA)

Fundamental Analysis

As its name suggests, fundamental analysis is the study of the underlying fundamentals of whatever we are trading. For example, if we are looking to trade IBM stock, fundamental analysis would have us look at things like:

Earnings reports: Is the company profitable? Are the profits or losses increasing or decreasing?

Market share: Is the company in a dominant position from which it can dictate prices, or is it at the mercy of bigger players?

Price to Earnings (p/e) ratios: A measure of how accurately the current share price represents the value of the company based on its current and projected earnings

New product launches: Are there potentially profitable new products on the horizon?

Relative sector performance: Is the company doing better or worse than its peers?

And so on...

Essentially we would be looking to find out as much about the company (or commodity, or whatever we were trading) as we possibly could, to form an opinion as to whether the current market *price* accurately reflected its *value.*

In the case of the IBM example we may look at all of the above, the current balance sheet, likely earnings for the next quarter and so on, add it all up and divide by the issued share capital (the number of shares in existence), and decide that IBM as a company is worth $95 per share.

If the actual current price were $90, we would have a valid reason to buy. There would be no guarantees that the price would move to $95 of course, a stock price only reflects *perceived value* — an important point to remember. However, if enough people came to the same conclusion as us and started buying up the stock, this would push the price higher (we'll look in more detail exactly why this is so later on).

Technical Analysis

Technical analysis is the study of graphs and charts of prices. Technical Analysis (TA) does not care what the underlying instrument is, in other words, whether it is a stock, a futures contract, or an interest rate bond, the principles remain the same.

TA is based on the idea that patterns can be found in price movements, and that these patterns have a tendency to repeat themselves,§ thus giving an opportunity to predict likely future direction of price.

Comparing The Two

Opinions vary on the two analysis methods, and proponents of one often go to great lengths to put down the other (Technical Analysts often refer to "Funnymentals"!)

For the purposes of our trading it is sufficient to say that Fundamental Analysis is best suited to a longer term buy and hold type strategy, and that Technical Analysis is well suited to short term moves. That's not to say each cannot be used in the other scenario, and indeed when we come to Part Three of this book, we will use some Fundamentals in our trading strategy.

Why We Will Use Mostly TA

Fundamental analysis will not help us predict the sort of short term intraday moves that we will be trading. TA on the other hand, is very good at this.

As day traders, TA offers us certain other advantages. We don't need to spend a great deal of time finding out about the stock we are about to trade, because TA works the same on all stocks. Indeed, TA works on any type of trading instrument. A chart is a chart, whatever it may be charting. Thus we can become proficient in TA and subsequently trade many different instruments, we don't need to become an expert in those instruments.

TA also works in any timeframe. Concepts we learn and practice in day trading can be used equally well in longer timeframes (like buy and hold) should we choose to do so.

CHAPTER 3 - TRADING INSTRUMENTS

"Not everything that can be counted counts, and not everything that counts can be counted."
Albert Einstein

What Is There Out There To Trade?

More than just stocks! In the main, there are the following types of trading instruments:

- Stocks (Shares)
- Futures
- Options
- Currencies
- Bonds
- CFDs
- Spread Bets

We'll look at each in turn, concentrating more on stocks and futures because as we'll see later on, those are going to be the most important to us.

Stocks (Shares)

You might here these referred to as stocks, shares, or equities — they are all the same thing. Shares in a company are exactly that; when you buy a share (stock) in a company you become a part owner of that company.

Companies list their stock on one ore more *stock exchanges*. There are many such exchanges around the world, examples you may have heard of include the London Stock Exchange (LSE), the New York Stock Exchange (NYSE), the NASDAQ, and the Deutsch Bourse.

In fact, almost every developed country in the world has at least one stock exchange. Whilst companies usually list themselves at an exchange in the country in which they are based, they are not obliged to do so. Many larger companies list on a number of different exchanges at the same time, making it easier for international investors to invest in them.

Stocks are bought and sold through a *broker*, who acts as an intermediary between the trader and the exchange, taking a commission for their trouble. We'll look more at brokers in a little while. A stock market is an open market, and under certain circumstances it is possible to buy stock through one broker and then sell it through another if we so desire.

Futures

Futures are a derivative product. That's a fancy term which means they are derived from some underlying asset such as a commodity (like corn, soya, or oil) or a financial indicator like a stock index (such as the FTSE 100, the Dow 30, or the S&P 500).

A futures contract is a contract between buyer and seller, for a seller to deliver to the buyer a certain quantity of the underlying asset at a future date, at a price agreed now. You might want to read that a couple of times to be sure to understand it!

Futures were originally developed to help farmers and merchants offset risks associated with the fluctuating supply and demand for produce. Let's look at an example. The price a crop farmer will receive for his cereal harvest will vary according to supply and demand. If the year is good and all farmers have done well, supply will be high so prices will be low. The farmer would probably like to be able to know what price he will get for his harvest long before harvest time. Likewise the merchant who is going to buy the crop will want to know how much he is going to have to pay in advance.

The merchant can therefore buy a futures contract for a specified quantity of cereal at a price agreed now. The contract has an expiry date, and when that date is reached, the seller (i.e. the farmer) must deliver the agreed quantity, regardless of what the value is at that time.

However, before the contract expires, the merchant can if he wishes, sell the contract on to a different merchant. If the price of cereal has risen since he purchased the contract, he could sell it to this other merchant for more than he paid for it, but less than the current price of the underlying cereal. Thus the original merchant makes a profit on the deal, and the new merchant gets his cereal for a better price than the current market price. For the farmer, nothing has changed. He will deliver his cereal to whoever holds the contract when it expires, he's already been paid. Everyone's happy.

As we can see, these contracts offer a great opportunity for trade, and a huge market has been created around them. These days it is possible to buy and sell futures contracts for all sorts of things, not just commodities. For example, we can trade contracts based on the value of the S&P 500 share index. Obviously when such a contract expires we cannot deliver "an S&P 500 share index" to the buyer, so we would have to deliver the cash equivalent.

To enable trading in indices like the S&P 500, such indices are valued at a *price per point*. The S&P 500 e-mini futures contract, for example, is valued at $50 per point. So if the index is at 1250, then its value is $62,500 (1250 x $50). If we buy a contract at this price, and the index subsequently rises to 1255 the contract is now worth $62,750, so we can sell it for a $250 profit. Again, we wouldn't actually need to be spending tens of thousands of dollars to buy the contract, we can do this with other people's money as we'll see later.

Index futures contracts usually expire every three months, normally at the end of March, June, September, and December. The contracts are traded on futures exchanges around the world, such as the Chicago Mercantile Exchange (CME), London International Futures and Options Exchange (LIFFE), the Chicago Board of Trade (CBOT), and the Eurex exchange. Each contract is a product of the exchange on which it is traded, thus a contract purchased on LIFFE for example, can only be sold back through LIFFE.

As with stocks, futures trading is carried out through a broker, who charges a commission.

Options

An Option allows the holder the right, but not the obligation, to acquire or to sell a predetermined quantity of stock or futures contracts, or a particular asset, at a fixed price, on or before a specified date, ending with the expiration date. That's another one you may want to read a couple of times!

Options are typically used in hedging, which is to say they may be bought or sold in the opposite direction to another trade in an effort to offset any losses should the main trade go against the trader.

Warning: options strategies can be (and usually are) complicated! They are beyond the scope of this book. It is sufficient to know that they exist, but we won't be using them.

Currencies

Currencies are traded in pairs. For example, we can buy dollars with pounds sterling, or euros with dollars. They may also be traded indirectly as futures contracts.

By buying one currency with another in a process called *forex* (FOReign EXchange), and then selling it back, it is possible to profit from ever changing exchange rates. Here's an example: The British Pound is valued at 1.61 US Dollars (i.e. one US Dollar is worth 62 pence). We buy 10,000 US Dollars, costing us £6,200.

The Pound weakens against the Dollar and is now worth $1.56 (i.e. one US Dollar is now worth just over 64 pence). We can sell back our 10,000 US Dollars for £6,400, giving us a profit of £200.

Clearly to make large profits we would need to be trading large sums of money, but we can get round this using other people's cash as we will see later (I know I've said that a few times, but don't worry, we are getting to it!) Typically in the forex market, currencies are traded in lots of 10,000. That means very small changes in exchange rates can mean big profits — and big losses.

The forex market is the biggest market in the world in terms of volume and value, with trillions of dollars worth of transactions occurring daily. It trades twenty four hours a day, five and a half days a week.

Bonds

Bonds are fixed interest assets typically issued for a period of more than one year by governments, banks, and other types of large institutions including corporations, who sell them to raise capital.

When a trader buys a bond, he or she is effectively lending money to the seller, who in turn agrees to repay the amount of the loan plus interest, at a specified time.

Typically, as equity prices rise, bond prices fall, and vice versa. Consequently bonds are often used in hedging.

CFDs

CFD stands for Contract For Difference. A CFD is a proprietary derivative instrument, a contract based on an underlying stock, index future, currency, or commodity. That means instead of buying, for example, stock in Amazon.com, we could buy a CFD which is a contract whose price is always the same as the stock price for Amazon.com. If the price of Amazon.com stock rises, we could sell our CFD at the new higher price, realising a profit.

CFDs are popular in the UK where they attract no stamp duty, unlike the underlying assets themselves. They aren't traded through brokers, but instead are bought and sold directly by the companies who create them. Because they are an entirely artificial product with no intrinsic value (they are little more than an idea linked to the price of something real), they cannot be bought from one company and sold to another.

There are usually no commission costs for trading CFDs, the companies who create, buy, and sell them, make their money in other ways.

As a final point on CFDs, it is important to note that whilst they are in theory based on the price of an underlying asset, be that a stock or a commodity or whatever, the companies that create them are usually under no obligation to match the asset price exactly. So if you are holding a CFD based on the price of oil for example, and the price of oil doubles overnight, the CFD company is not obliged to price their CFD at the new high price. Of course, it is in their interests to do so otherwise their reputation will be short lived, as will their business! But it is something to bear in mind nonetheless.

Spread Bets

Spread bets are exactly the same thing as CFDs, but by calling the product a spread bet, UK tax laws mean any profits made trading them are not subject to any form of tax (note: tax laws can and do change, be sure to take independent advice from a qualified tax advisor before trading spread bet products). Consequently spread bets are very popular in the UK.

Spread betting offers a similar range of underlying instruments to CFDs. They are almost always offered through the same companies as CFDs, and like CFDs, there is no obligation on the company offering the spread bet product to match the underlying asset price exactly.

Unfortunately spread betting is not generally available to US residents due to American trading laws.

We will look at CFDs and spread bets again in Part Three, they provide a useful way to start trading the markets with a small amount of capital.

Trading With Other People's Money

I've mentioned a few times that we can trade using other peoples money, so it's about time we examined this idea in a bit more detail. Trading on *margin* allows us to use our capital as a deposit on the stock (or futures contract, CFD, commodity etc) that we wish to buy. Our broker will put up the rest of the cash required for a trade transaction as a short term loan. To put it another way, they provide most of the money for the trade.

The margin is the amount of cash we need in our account to cover the value of the transaction. There are two kinds of margin:

Initial Margin - the percentage amount we need in order to open a new position (i.e. to actually buy or sell the stock we want).

Overnight Margin - the amount of margin we need to maintain to keep our position open overnight. This amount will be higher, because prices can fluctuate greatly overnight and our broker needs to make sure we have adequate funds to cover any losses that may occur due to price moves against us. As day traders we never hold overnight, so this second kind of margin can be largely ignored.

Margin requirements vary from broker to broker, and between markets. Trading shares on the NASDAQ exchange for example, the maximum margin is 4:1, which means we can spend four times as much as we have in our account. Or looked at another way, our broker will put up three quarters of the cash required for our trade. Spread Bet and CFD firms often allow much higher margin, as much as 20:1 in some cases.

Currencies are traded with even higher margin, 100:1 or more. This is because currency movements are relatively very small, so to profit from them it is necessary to buy and sell in huge quantities.

If we are holding a margined position and it moves against us to such a degree that were we to liquidate it, we would no longer have enough cash in our trading account to meet the margin requirement, our broker will issue a *margin call* for more funds to be deposited to make up the shortfall. Some brokers will immediately liquidate some or all of the position in order to protect themselves.

Margin therefore gives us the ability to leverage our capital for greater percentage returns. Of course, in doing so it also exposes us to greater risk.

Here's a worked example to illustrate the use of margin. Let us imagine that we want to buy 1000 NASDAQ shares, currently priced at $35.50 each. The total cost is $35.50 x 1000 = $35,500

Our broker gives us the full 4:1 margin allowed on the NASDAQ, which means we need a quarter of the purchase price in order to cover the purchase. $35,500 / 4 = $8,875. So the Initial Margin on the purchase is $8,875.

The broker will only accept the trade if we have enough funds in the account to cover the margin, and will allocate those funds so they cannot be used again elsewhere whilst the position is open. So if our account balance is $10,000, then on allocating the $8,875 margin for the new position, the remaining available balance is $1,125. In other words, the money in our account that we can actually use to open further positions is now $1,125.

If the price of the stock fell to $34.50, the margin required to cover our trade would also fall. 1000 shares x $34.50 = $34,500, which divided by 4 (4:1 margin) = $8,625. However, because our unrealised profit and loss is updated in real time, the available balance in our account is now much lower. Unrealised profit and loss is that which has yet to become real by liquidating the position. So in this example, if we now sold the stock at the new price of $34.50, we would get back $34,500 for it, which is a loss of $1000. Another way of putting this is that the price fell $1 per share, and we hold 1000 shares so have lost $1000. Thus our account balance is now $9000. If we take out the current margin requirement of $8,625, our available balance is now just $375.

If the price fell much further, our available balance would become negative and the broker would issue a margin call meaning we would need to deposit further funds in the account to keep the position open. If on the other hand, the price went our way and showed a profit, our available balance would increase.

CHAPTER 4 - THE MARKET

"The thing that most affects the stock market is everything."
James Palysted Wood

Defining The Market

We talk about this thing *the market*, but what actually is it? There are lots of markets: the stock market, the futures market, the currency market, and more. Just like the weekly grocery market in town, these financial markets are where people meet to buy and sell various products.

Any market is made up of the people trading it. With the exception of currencies, spread bets and CFDs, financial products are bought and sold through an exchange. This is a place where buyers and sellers trade with each other. The exchange takes a small fee for matching a buyer with a seller and enabling the transaction. There are different types of trader: Institutions, Market Makers, Retail Traders / Investors. Not all of them participate in every market. It is the actions of these participants that make the market. Let's look at the differences between them.

Institutions

The institutions are the big boys, the likes of Morgan Stanley, Goldman Sachs, the banks like Deutsch Bank, Bank of America, and their kin. Lehman Brothers, until their demise, were another example of an institution These guys trade their clients accounts, their clients being pension funds, hedge funds, investment funds, and particularly wealthy individuals.

The institutions trade in most markets, and usually deal directly with the exchange. They move huge sums of money around, which can be a disadvantage to them because they cannot fill a massive order without moving the price of whatever they are buying or selling, against themselves (we'll see why later).

Market Makers (MMs)

These are also institutional players, and are again the likes of Goldman Sachs, UBS, etc They deal in the equities and futures markets. The traditional role of a market maker is to provide liquidity in a stock. That simply means they are there to ensure that there is always somebody to take the opposite side of any trade. In the past on the London Stock Exchange (LSE), all trading was done through MMs. They would sell to buyers, and buy from sellers, moving the price of a stock accordingly to attract equal numbers of each. Some LSE shares (non SETS shares) are still traded this way. MMs also deal directly through the exchange.

Retail Traders / Investors

These are the little people like you and me, individuals buying and selling for investment or short term profit. Because retail traders trade in relatively tiny amounts, it's not viable for them to deal directly with the exchange. Thus trading is carried out via a broker who takes the order from the customer and executes it through the exchange. The broker also takes a small fee for handling this transaction.

Market Price Information

Before we can buy or sell any stock (or indeed anything at all), we need to know how much it costs. Given that a large part of our job as traders is to try and predict whether the prices of stocks are going to rise or fall, we need to fully understand where these prices come from and what makes them move.

Prices

As with any other type of product, financial products have a price. In fact, financial products like stocks have two prices, these are called the bid and the ask (sometimes known as the offer).

Bid prices are prices at which market participants are willing to *buy* the financial product. *Ask* (or *offer*) prices are the prices at which market participants are willing to *sell* the product.

There can be lots of bid prices, and lots of ask prices, because different market participants are willing to buy or sell at different prices. Those we usually get to see are the best bid and the best ask, the most attractive prices available at the given time. Here's an example. For stock in a company called AnyCo, there are people queuing up to buy and sell at the following prices.

BID	ASK
$85.20	$85.25
$85.19	$85.26
$85.17	$85.27
$85.10	$85.30

In the table we can see people lining up on the left to buy the stock, and on the right to sell it. The lowest price offered (i.e. the person willing to sell at the lowest price) is $85.25 so this is the best ask. The highest price being bid (i.e. the person willing to pay the most for the stock) is $85.20, so this is the best bid. The difference between these two prices is called the *spread*, so in this example the spread is 5 cents.

In all markets we could try and buy directly from the person offering the best ask, and sell directly to the person bidding the best bid. Thus in simple terms we could look at the top two numbers and say that the bid price is the price we can sell at, and the ask price is the price we can buy at.

Once all of the available stock at a particular price has been bought or sold, the best bid or best ask becomes the next available on the list. So in the example, if we purchased all the stock being offered at $85.25, the next best ask would be $85.26. This is how the prices we see, move up and down.

If we buy directly at the ask, and plan to sell directly at the bid, we would need to wait for the price to rise by the value of the spread before we could close our position at break even. In the above example, if we bought at $85.25, the best bid price would need to go up by 5 cents before we could sell at break even (not counting any commission we would be paying the broker for the transactions).

In some markets though, we have the ability to directly place our own buy or sell orders in this queue of orders. So in our example we could place an order to buy at a price of $85.21. This would instantly become the best bid price and therefore would go to the top of the list. If someone wanted to sell, we would be the first person they could sell to and so we would buy their stock at the price we wanted. This reduces the spread; assuming no new orders were entered, the best bid would now be $85.20 so the price now need move only 1 cent for us to be able to close our position at break even.

A table of available prices like the one above, is called the *market depth*. We will see as we progress that not all markets make this market depth information available to traders, and on those that do, it is optional whether or not we can see it. We will also see that the information in it can be misleading!

Size

When traders place orders to buy or sell, they don't just specify which stock they want and the price, they must also specify the quantity they want to buy or are offering to sell. On the market depth screen there are more columns for Size. Let's expand on our AnyCo example.

Size	BID	ASK	Size
100	**$85.20**	**$85.25**	**200**
500	$85.19	$85.26	1000
500	$85.17	$85.27	1000
200	$85.10	$85.30	1000

Here we can see that the best bidder is willing to buy 100 shares, and there are 200 shares available at the best ask. We can also see that at the next levels in the market depth there is far more stock offered for sale than there are people bidding to buy. This is a clue that the price may be set to fall, or already falling. The bias is clearly to the downside. It is only a clue though, nothing in trading is ever clear-cut one hundred percent fact. For example all those people offering the thousands of shares for sale could decide to pull (cancel) their orders.

Another way of looking at this information is that the people on the ask side presumably think the price is going to go high enough for their order to be filled, which could therefore indicate a rising price. So we can see that a simple snap-shot of one moment in time does not provide enough information to form an opinion, rather it is necessary to observe the market over time.

Last Price & Size

When viewing price information, we will usually be able to see the best bid and best ask prices and sizes. We are normally (depending on the market we are trading) also able to see the last price and size. This is the price and size of the most recent trade to occur.

So for example, a typical set of market data might look like this:

Size	BID	ASK	Size	Last	Size
50	$85.20	$85.25	200	**$85.20**	**50**

The last price and size fields are showing us that the last trade to occur was 50 shares at $85.20. If this was the same stock as the previous examples, and we had been watching these prices, we would conclude from this information that this trade was somebody buying from the best bidder.

By continuing to watch this information alone, you can see that it would be possible to get an idea as to the direction of this stock's price. For example, if we continued to see lots of last trades occurring at the bid price, and they heavily outnumbered the trades that went through at the ask price, we could assume that at this time more people wanted to sell and the price was falling, or likely to fall in the immediate future.

Clearly in a fast moving market with many thousands of trades going through all day, it is not feasible to be continually watching this price information for every stock that we might want to trade. We need some way of summarising what has happened in the past to help us form an opinion of what might happen in the future. This is where the chart comes to our rescue.

CHAPTER 5 - CHARTING INTRODUCTION

"Un croquis vaut mieux qu'un long discours." *("A picture is worth a thousand words.")*
Napoleon

Why Use Charts?

The chart is the core tool of technical analysis. We use charts to summarise historical price information in a graphical way.

The market is a constant struggle between buyers (known in stock market terminology as *bulls*) and sellers (*bears*). A price chart summarises this constant pulling of price up and down by the bulls and the bears. By looking at what a stock price has done in the past we can gain clues about what it may do in the future. How is this possible? Because prices are driven by people, and people are creatures of habit. We find many different patterns on charts that repeat themselves time and again. We can use these patterns to predict probable future price movements.

Another way to think about this is that because prices are driven the actions of large numbers of people, trading is all about crowd psychology. When we look at a price chart for a stock, we are really looking at the collective psychology of the people trading that stock — their hope, fear, and greed. It is important to bear this in mind when trading. The market is the group of people who are trading the same stock. If we know what drives the majority, and can remain emotionally detached ourselves, we can be one step ahead of the crowd, and that means we can profit from their fear and greed.

Because there are players in the market who are trading in various different timeframes (i.e. people holding a stock from a few minutes right up to those holding for maybe many years), the crowd psychology works in all of those timeframes. Thus price charts also work in all timeframes. We can find the same patterns when we look at a chart summarising price information for a period of one hour as a chart summarising information for a year.

Bar Charts

In standard price charts, bars are used to summarise a period of trading activity. A single bar might summarise trades that have taken place in a one minute period, through to a one day period or more.

The basic information contained in any price bar is:

- The Open - the price at the start of the time period covered by the bar
- The Close - the price at the end of the period
- The High - the highest price that was reached throughout the duration of the bar
- The Low - the lowest price reached in the period

While it is perfectly possible to chart bid or ask prices, we generally chart the last price as this means a chart is showing where trades actually occurred, not where they *could* have occurred.

Let's look at an example bar in more detail:

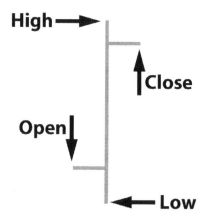

We can add a scale to this bar:

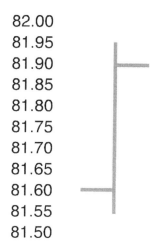

82.00
81.95
81.90
81.85
81.80
81.75
81.70
81.65
81.60
81.55
81.50

We see here that at the start of the time period covered by this bar, the price was 81.60, and that at the end it was 81.90. At some point in-between, the price fell to 81.55, and rose to 81.95.

It's clear that because a bar is only a summary, there are limitations to the information it displays. For example, we don't know in the bar above if the price opened at 81.60, dipped to 81.55 then rose to 81.95 before dropping to 81.90 at the close, or if it opened and rose straight up to 81.95 before dropping right back down. In other words, if we were to see how the bar was formed, it might look like this:

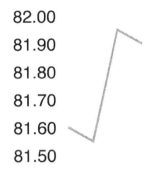

Or this:

Or even this:

We must be careful about the conclusions we draw from an individual bar. What we can safely say in this example, is that at the end of the period the price was higher than at the start. We can deduce that there were more people wanting to buy than to sell, pushing the price higher.

On its own an individual bar won't give us many clues about the immediate direction of the price. We might assume from the above bar that as it seems the bulls were in control, the price is likely to rise. Putting the bar in context of those before it will give us more to work with (our bar is the one circled):

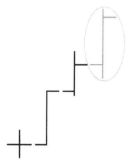

Taken in the context above, we can see that over the course of the four bars the price is steadily rising. This might give us more reason to believe the price will continue to rise. In this next example however, it would appear the price has been steadily falling, but our bar at the end shows a possible change in direction:

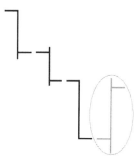

So the same bar might lead us to different conclusions depending on the preceding bars. Now consider the following bar:

In this bar we can see that quite a struggle ensued between buyers and sellers, but at the end of the period the bears (sellers) managed to bring the price right back to where it was at the open. Again, the significance of this bar could be seen differently in different situations:

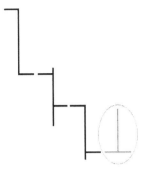

Here prices are clearly falling. In the last bar, the bulls have made a valiant effort to push the price up, but in the end they have been overcome by the bears who have brought it back down. Our conclusion here might be that having won this struggle, they will be able to continue to push the price lower in the next bar and that the downwards trend is likely to continue.

In this example, the price has been rising steadily:

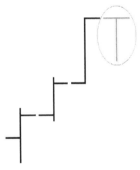

Our bar at the end suggests that the bulls who have been pushing the price up, were finally overcome by the bears. In other words, the price got to a point where there were more people wanting to sell than wanting to buy. The sellers overwhelmed the buyers and the price closed at the low of the period. So we might conclude that having become the dominant force, the sellers will push the price lower still. Consequently if we were holding this share, we may consider selling it at this point. Here's another important bar, it's called a Doji:

This is a classic sign of indecision. It doesn't matter where this bar occurs, it simply shows that there was no overall control between buyers and sellers. If we were holding a share and encountered this bar we may want to be more cautious and watch what happens next closely, as it could be that the direction is about to change.

It is important to realise that a bar on its own gives you no indication as to the size of the trades that were taking place. It is possible for a *rogue trade* to occur some distance from the main price action and cause a bar to look distorted:

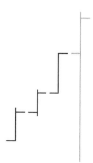

In the set of bars above we have no way of knowing if there was suddenly a huge amount of selling activity in the last bar (followed by an even larger amount of buying to push the price back up to where it closed), or if there was a single trade of 10 shares that occurred way below the rest of the action. It could even be that a trade was misreported by the exchange, and this bar shows an error in the data they provide, although most exchanges now send corrections if such errors occur.

Japanese Candlesticks

Candlesticks are a different way of illustrating the same information contained in a price bar. They are very popular because many people find them easier to read. Whole books have been written on the subject of candlestick charting and the recognition of patterns made by groups of candles. These patterns are the same whether made by bars or candles; the choice of which to use on a chart is purely down to personal preference.

A candlestick consists of a wide body (sometimes called the real body) and a thin wick (sometimes called the shadow). The top of the wick indicates the high, and the bottom of the wick the low. The top and bottom of the body indicate the open and close. If the candle body is solid, then the top is the open and the bottom the close (i.e. the price dropped in the period of the candle). In a candle that is not solid, the bottom of the body marks the open, and the top the close (i.e. the price rose in that period). Some traders prefer to use red and green coloured candles in place of filled in and empty candles. Again, it all comes down to personal preference. Here are some examples. This candle represents a price that rose during the period it covers. It could also be represented as a solid green candle:

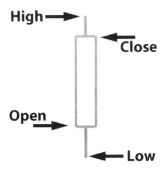

Here is a candle showing a price that fell during the period it covered:

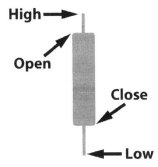

Here are some candles and bars compared side by side:

As we can see, the information shown by candles and bars is identical.

Volume

Volume tells us the quantity (of stock, or futures contracts, or pork bellies, or grapefruit etc) that have been traded in the period covered by a bar or candle. When we add it to a chart it is normally shown at the bottom, with one bar of volume for every price bar.

Volume can be very useful for indicating the end of a trend. In the above example we can see that as the price was nearing its high point, there was a peak in volume. This volume was caused by a large number of sellers coming into the market and overwhelming the buyers, thus arresting the rise in price. The next bars showed a decrease in price and a decrease in volume, which suggests that the buyers had walked away and that sellers were now driving the price. Indeed, as can be seen, the price continued to fall.

We can also use volume to try and get round the sticky problem of those rogue trades I mentioned earlier. In the example, we couldn't tell if the very long bar was caused by a solitary trade happening at a strange price, or massive selling and buying action driving the price way down and back up again. Adding volume to the chart would give us an extra clue. If massive buying and selling was going on, we would see it in a correspondingly large volume bar.

Other Chart Types

It is worth mentioning briefly that bar and candle charts are not the only game in town. Other methods of charting include:

Lines - these are the very basic charts often used by newspapers and TV shows when illustrating a simple summary of price action. They plot only closing prices, and are useful for getting a very quick idea of longer term price history. Their simplicity means they're not suitable for trading from as far as we are concerned.

Tick Charts - in these charts a bar (or candle) represents a summary of the trading activity that occurred within a certain number of trades instead of in a certain time period. For example, a trader may elect to have the chart start a new bar after every 100 trades that have occurred. This effectively does away with the time axis, and can give a more consistent view of the market between busy and quiet periods. Tick charts are frequently used by very short term traders who are looking to capture a high number of exceptionally small price movements (scalpers).

Point & Figure - this is the oldest form of price charting. It was developed long before computers were around, and therefore Point and Figure charts are designed to be drawn up by hand. They are a completely different way of graphically plotting price action, and do away with the time axis altogether. They are more suited to long term trading, although there are some day trading strategies that make use of this type of chart.

Further alternative chart types include Kagi, Point Break, and Renko charts. We will be using standard time based bar and candlestick charts for the rest of this book.

Chapter 6 - Technical Analysis Basics

"There are no facts, only interpretations."
Friedrich Nietzsche

Now we know where prices come from, and how we can summarise them on charts. The next step is to be able to analyse those charts in order that we can try and form our opinion of where the price is likely to go next. Time to get into Technical Analysis! Don't worry, the name might make it sound like you need a math degree to understand it, but it's actually very straightforward. If you can tell the difference between a circle, a square, and a triangle, you should be just fine with Technical Analysis.

Support and Resistance

Support and resistance forms the basis of all Technical Analysis (TA). Some definitions are now in order:

- *Support* is any point at which a falling price meets enough buyers to arrest the fall.
- *Resistance* is any point at which a rising price meets enough sellers to halt the rise.

The more times a price meets support or resistance at the same level, the more significant that support or resistance is. Enough talk, here's an example of support:

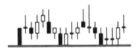

In this stock chart segment we can see the price is falling. It meets Support at the point indicated by the horizontal line I've drawn in, and then rises again. The second time it drops, it again meets support at the same price level as a number of buyers move in and overwhelm the sellers. This then happens a third time, so by now we can see that this is quite a significant support level.

What's making this happen? Obviously not everyone trading this stock can see the line I've drawn on the chart, so why is the price repeatedly "bouncing" off it? Quite simply, each time the price approaches that level, there are enough buyers around who think that it won't go any lower, so they're buying up stock in sufficient quantities to push the price back up.

This is the group psychology I mentioned earlier. Enough people have the same opinion that collectively they are causing the price to change direction at the same place. What's really cool is that if this happens a few times, more people will notice, and will draw the same conclusion, meaning even more potential buyers at the support price. It's a kind of self-fulfilling prophecy.

Eventually though, the buyers who are buying at that price will become fewer in number as their orders are filled. At some point there may not be enough buyers left to stop the price falling through that price level, and the support will be broken.

If this happens, many of the earlier buyers will see the price drop and will decide to sell their holding immediately, before their position moves further into loss. This selling will cause the price to drop further, and faster.

Similarly, many of the traders who were already holding the stock will know that this break is likely to cause the price to drop, and so they too will sell their holding, thus adding further to the selling pressure and the price fall.

The traders who were previously buying at the support level before it was broken, are now sitting on a potential loss. If the price goes back up to what was the support level, they will see this as an opportunity to sell their holding at or close to the price they paid for it (i.e. break even). This selling will cause the price to fall again.

Also, many traders who were already holding stock before the price broke the support level and didn't sell it immediately, will also want to sell if and when the price gets back there, so adding yet more to the selling pressure and making the price even more likely to fall.

All of this selling going on at the previous support level means that the support has now turned into resistance! Every time the price tries to rise, more selling happens, forcing it back down.

This is actually a very common occurrence. Exactly the same thing can happen in reverse, with a resistance level turning into support.

Let's look at what happened next in the previous example. We can see that indeed the fourth time the price reached the support level, it broke through:

The support immediately turned into resistance, and the price tried several times to go up through it but was met with selling pressure which drove it back down. Eventually the buyers gave up and the price fell away rapidly.

As a rule of thumb, if a price fails to break a support or resistance level by the fourth attempt, it is likely to reverse (but remember, nothing is ever certain in trading!) A break of support or resistance (a *breakout*) may not always carry through. Sometimes the price will breakout and then quickly reverse. This is often called a false break, or a fakeout.

Support and resistance lines are not necessarily as absolute as in the above examples. A support line might be drawn at roughly a certain price, maybe the price bounces within a few cents of the same level each time. When looking for support and resistance you need to use your judgement to a certain extent. Think about the group psychology, remember that those price movements are caused by real people. If a support line looks obvious to you, it must look obvious to an awful lot of other people who are watching, and that alone means it has some authority.

Volume can be used as a confirming indicator of a breakout from support or resistance. If a break is accompanied by a rise in volume, it is more likely to carry through. A break on thin volume on the other hand, may indicate that just one or two small trades have occurred the other side of the support or resistance level, but that on the whole it is still holding.

Trends

Trends can be thought of as support and resistance on a slope. An up-trend is formed when the price makes higher highs and higher lows — i.e. the price is continually rising over time. A down-trend is formed when the price makes lower highs and lower lows — i.e. the price is continually falling over time.

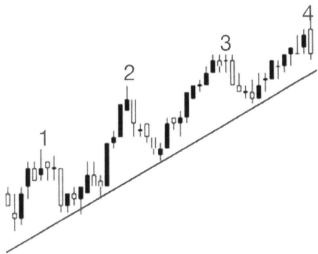

The highs and lows I'm talking about here are the points where the price sets a new extreme value. In other words, a high would be a candle where those either side of it show lower prices, and vice versa for a low. In the up-trend example here, you can see four clearly defined highs, numbered.

Here's an example down-trend. We can draw *trend lines* on a trend by linking the lows in an up-trend, or the highs in a down-trend. You can see trend lines drawn in on the previous examples.

Just as with regular horizontal support and resistance, the more times the price touches a trend line and bounces off, the more authority the trend line is said to have. And again like regular support and resistance lines, a trend line doesn't have to be absolute, we can allow the price some wiggle room around it.

A common mantra among traders is *"Let the trend be your friend!"* If we are trading long (buying and hoping to sell at a higher price), we have more chance of success if we do so in an up-trend, and vice versa when trading short. So for example, a simple and low risk trading strategy could be to sell short when the price bounces off a trend line in a down-trend. The momentum of the trend means there is a higher probability of the price continuing to fall. Similarly, we could buy long when the price bounces off a trend line in an up-trend.

Trying to pick the end of a trend and trade in the opposite direction (known as top and bottom picking) is a high risk strategy. Trends by their very definition, spend more time trending that they do changing direction (something that they can only do once!) So by simply trading in the same direction as the trend, we are already putting ourselves on the side of greater probability.

Unfortunately markets only trend around 20% of the time on average. The rest of the time they will oscillate more or less sideways. In such sideways movement we cannot necessarily tell if the price has a higher probability of starting a new up-trend or down-trend, so entering trades would be higher risk. We are much better off waiting for a new trend to become established and then trading in line with that trend.

Trends are simply rising or falling support and resistance lines. As such, a trend line will eventually be broken. Often just before the breakout, the price will stay very close to the line as the buyers (or sellers in a down-trend) start to run out of steam. Let's look at an example (note the example is an up-trend, but the same ideas apply equally in reverse to down-trends).

In this example, the price touches the line a couple of times, then runs along it before breaking through. The breakout may or may not carry through (volume might give us a clue here). If it doesn't, it may be possible to draw a new trend line taking into account the price action where the breakout occurred. Looking at what happened next in this example, we can see that we could draw in a new line to encompass the new price movement:

Because an up-trend line is effectively a rising support line, it will often turn into resistance once broken. In the above example after the break of the new line, the price comes up and bounces off the trend line before falling away sharply. Looking further, we can also see some regular horizontal support:

Very often after a trend line is broken, the price will enter a period of consolidation where it moves up and down within a confined range (sideways oscillation), before either continuing its original trend, or trending in the opposite direction.

Simple Patterns

In addition to trend, support, and resistance (sometimes referred to collectively as TSR), there are a number of common patterns that can be found on price charts. These fall into two categories: 1) Continuation patterns, which indicate the trend is likely to continue after a pause. 2) Reversal patterns, which indicate the trend is likely to change direction after a pause.

When a market is trending, it often needs to stop for breath. When this happens a continuation pattern may form, and this pattern can give us a clue when the trend might start again, and how far it will run. Some continuation patterns are also reversal patterns!

Let's take a look at these patterns. We'll see each one first as a simplified line diagram to help you see the overall shape, and then as an actual candlestick chart example. Real life charts rarely make textbook patterns, we are looking for the right shape rather than a perfect pattern every time.

Rectangles

A rectangle is made by the price moving sideways between resistance and support, before continuing its move upwards or downwards. When the price breaks out of a rectangle (i.e. it breaks the support or resistance level), it will usually do so in the direction of the original trend, but bear in mind it may break the other way, so we always wait for the breakout to occur before trading the pattern. A rectangle pattern in a down-trend would look like this:

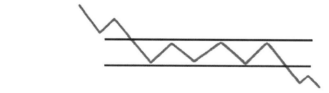

Here's a real chart example. In this example, a low risk trade would be to short sell the stock once the price has broken out of the rectangle. The price was already falling so there is a good probability that it will fall further having broken below the support line.

Flags

Flags are rectangles on a slope in the opposite direction to the trend. When a flag is forming, we have no way of knowing if it is going to be a flag, or if it is in fact a new trend in the other direction, so of course we must wait for it to break out before we enter a new trade based upon it.

The part of the trend up to (or down to) the start of the flag itself is called the flag pole. When the flag breaks out, the price will often continue for the same distance as this flag pole before entering its next consolidation phase. A flag pattern in an up-trend looks like this:

Here's a real chart example:

In this example the price has been moving upwards, then *retraces* (backtracks) some way in a flag pattern as it catches its breath. A low risk trade would be to buy stock once the price broke above the down-trend line that forms the top of the flag (marked 1 on the chart). There is good probability that the price will continue to rise, and indeed we can reasonably hope that the rise will be of the same magnitude as that of the price rise leading up to the start of the flag pattern.

Triangles

Triangles can be continuation or reversal patterns. They are similar to rectangles, but the support and / or resistance lines that contain the price are trend lines.

What is actually happening in a triangle is the buyers are trying to push the price up and the sellers are trying to pull it down. As time goes on each side is becoming more cautious, and the movements in either direction are becoming smaller and smaller. Eventually one side may win and the price will break out of the triangle, often with great force as the pent up buying or selling energy is released.

Because one or both sides of the triangle may be a trend line, there are three types of triangle pattern that can occur:

- *Ascending triangles* - the resistance line at the top is horizontal, and the support line is an up-trend line.
- *Descending triangles* - the opposite.
- *Symmetrical triangles* - both the support and resistance lines are trend lines.

Ascending triangles are more likely to break out to the up-side (but not always). This is even more likely if they occur in an up-trend. Descending triangles are more likely to break out to the down-side (but not always). Again, this is even more likely in a down-trend. Symmetrical triangles are most likely to break out in the direction of the original trend, but not always (nothing is ever certain!) As with rectangles, because the break could occur in either direction, we must wait for it to occur before trading it.

For a breakout to carry any weight it should ideally occur no later than three quarters of the way along the triangle — i.e. if you were to extend the triangle lines until they met, the price should break out before one quarter distance from the apex. If the price breaks out after this point, the chances are it is because the price has now entered a sideways phase rather than because buyers or sellers have pushed it outside of the pattern. In other words, the price isn't in a triangle pattern any more.

The distance from the top of the triangle to the bottom, at its widest point, can be used to measure the likely distance the price will travel if and when it breaks out. Let's look at some examples of the different kind of triangles you can expect to see, starting with a symmetrical triangle:

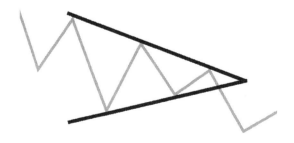

Here's a real chart example of a symmetrical triangle in a down-trend. Note that the distance between the top and bottom of the triangle at its widest point (shown here by the marker) gives a target for how far the price will move when (if) it breaks out of the pattern:

Here's what an ascending triangle pattern looks like:

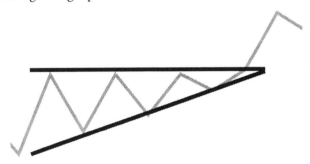

Now let's have a look at a real chart example, this time in an up trend. The same price target criteria apply as above, again the marker shows the prediction for the price move after the breakout.

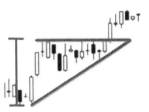

Here's a descending triangle:

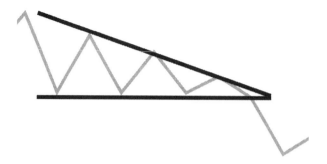

And a real chart example:

Triangles are one of the most reliable and easy to spot patterns. This makes them a favourite among traders, which in itself reinforces their reliability and ubiquity (that self-fulling group psychology again). I know traders whose entire trading strategy is simply to look for triangle patterns and trade them when they break out. I think we can do a little better, and I'll show you how in Part Three of this book. But if you want to practice looking at real charts right now, you could do a lot worse than start looking for triangles.

Double Tops & Bottoms

Double tops and double bottoms are both reversal patterns, in other words, they signal a change in direction of the price trend. In a double top the price makes a high then falls back. It then tries to make another high, but fails to break above the previous one. This suggests that the sellers have come into the market in sufficient numbers to overwhelm the buyers, and the price will fall.

As with triangles and flags, the double top (and its equivalent in a falling market, the double bottom) can be predictive. The resulting fall is often the same size the height of the pattern. These patterns are more likely to work if the second high is slightly lower than the first, as this indicates the buyers are weakening.

Here's an example:

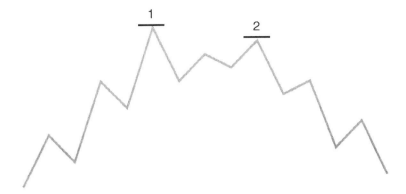

The price is making new highs, but high number 2 is lower than high number 1, suggesting sellers are gaining control and the up trend may be reversing.

Here's a real chart example:

In this example we see the price in a clear up-trend, making a series of higher highs and higher lows. After the high labelled 1, the price fails to make a higher low; this is the first clue that the trend may be coming to an end. The second circle shows where the price then makes a lower high. The pattern is confirmed when the price falls below the previous two lows (i.e. breaks the support). The distance between this support and the highest high may predict how far the price will now fall before consolidating. You may notice that in this example the pattern is also a descending triangle.

Head & Shoulders

A Head and Shoulders is another reversal pattern. It can be thought of as a triple top (or bottom). In a head and shoulders pattern the price makes a high, then a higher high, then a lower high, but with the lows around the same level:

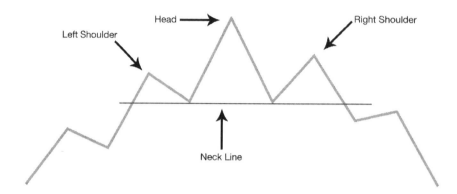

The head and shoulders can also be predictive in the same way as a double top or bottom. The pattern works equally in reverse, indicating the change from a down-trend to an up-trend.

Here's a real chart example:

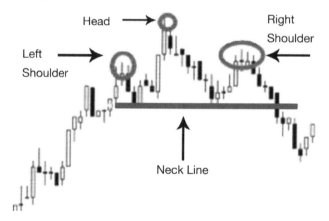

Again, the price is in a clear up-trend. It makes a high as indicated by the first circle (the left shoulder), then makes a higher low. After making the second high in the second circle (the head), the price comes down again and fails to make a higher low, giving us a clue that a double top or head and shoulders pattern might be forming. Finally the right shoulder is made by the third high, which is lower than the head. The pattern is confirmed when the support formed by the two previous lows (the neck line) is broken. The distance between the neck line and the top of the head may give an indication of how far the price will fall before it next consolidates.

Summary

In basic technical analysis, we are continually looking at support, resistance, trends, and patterns to give us clues about what the price might do next.

We can never know for sure where the price will go, but we can use the clues the charts give us to make an educated guess, and plan our trading accordingly. When the price confirms one way or another what it is doing, we will be ready to put that plan into action.

Our plan might be to enter a new trade if we don't have a position, or to get out of a trade if we think the move we are trading has come to an end or has not gone our way. Or it might simply be to wait and stay out of the market. It is important to remember that the market spends a lot of time going sideways, and that's not good for profits. We want to wait for the best high probability trades to come along, be ready to take them when they do, and equally ready to jump out of them when they don't work out.

Like everything else, chart reading takes practice. It's more of an art form than a science. Patterns rarely form exactly like textbook examples, they often have rough edges and it can take time to recognise them.

On the other hand, if you have to spend too long looking at a chart to find a pattern, it's most likely because it's not there! Beware of *squinting* — trying to make out patterns that aren't really there. The best chart patterns are the ones that leap out at you. If it's obvious to you, it should be obvious to everyone else looking at the same chart, and therefore has more chance of success.

Starting today, make a point of looking at real stock charts every day. You can find free charts at `http://finance.yahoo.com` or `http://www.google.com/finance`. Set them up to show bars or candlesticks, and then look for support and resistance lines, and patterns. If you have a printer, print some out and physically draw the lines and patterns on, it will really help you spot them. The more charts you look at, the better you will get at *reading* them.

CHAPTER 7 - INDICATORS

"While we are postponing, life speeds on."
Seneca

What Are Indicators?

Indicators are values that can be added to a price chart, other than the price itself (although the price can also be considered an indicator). Volume is one indicator that we have already looked at. Other indicators fall into two main categories, *moving average* based indicators, and *oscillators* or momentum indicators.

Indicators can be used individually, but are more commonly combined to give signals to buy or sell. Some traders trade only based on indicators, others don't use them at all. We will look briefly at some common indicators because it's important to understand the tools that are available. However, they will not play a large part in the final trading strategy that we are going to employ.

Moving Averages

Moving averages (MAs) are probably the oldest and simplest indicator, and also one of the most effective. A moving average is exactly what its name suggests — an average price that moves. It works by taking the closing prices of the last *n* bars (where *n* can be any number), adding them together, and dividing by *n* to give the average price over that period. The value is plotted on the price chart, and over time forms a line. The smaller the value for *n*, the quicker the average will react to the current price. Here's what an MA looks like:

This is a 10 period simple moving average. A basic way to trade from moving averages is to buy when the price crosses above them, and sell when it crosses below. However, whilst this certainly makes money in a trending market, in a sideways one the price *whipsaws* backwards and forwards over the MA. This chopping action leads to lots of small losing trades. We already know that prices only trend around 20% of the time, so this simple strategy is never likely to be a big winner.

A different way of using MAs as the basis of a trading system is to plot two or more with different *n* values on the same chart, and use the points where they cross as buy and sell signals. Here's the same chart as the previous example, but with a 15 period MA added (the bottom line):

Because it averages more price periods (candles), it is a slower average. The crossing of a fast average over a slower one can be used as a trading signal. By tuning the MAs, using two in this way can cut down on the number of whipsaws, but at the expense of missing some of the move in a trend.

Adding a layer of complexity, exponential moving averages (EMAs) and weighted moving averages (WMAs), weight prices so that the most recent carry more value than the older ones. This leads to an MA which more closely follows the price, in other words the moving average reacts faster to price changes.

In the next chart there is a 10MA and a 10EMA. You can see that whilst there isn't a huge difference, the EMA is quicker to react to changes in the price, with the regular simple moving average lagging behind.

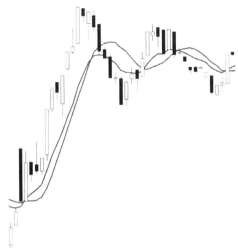

Like most aspects of technical analysis, moving averages have a degree of self fulfilling prophecy. If enough people are looking at the same thing, then they will expect the same thing to happen at the same time, react to it in the same way, and therefore make that expected outcome actually occur!

Because of this predictable crowd behaviour towards them, MAs can become variable lines of support and resistance. Looking back at the last example we see that halfway through the up-trend the price came down, touched the MA, and then bounced off continuing its rise. So the MA itself actually provided (or became) support. It's no coincidence that the bounce off the MA also occurred at a point where both the simple moving average and the exponential moving average coincided. Traders watching either one will have seen — and traded — the bounce, adding more weight to it.

That gives us yet another possible way of trading from moving averages. In the above example a low risk trade would be to have bought when the price bounced off the MA and continued in the direction of the established up-trend. If the price failed to go higher but instead broke down through the MA, we would quickly know that the trade wasn't working out and could exit with as small a loss as possible.

Because moving averages work well in trends, they can provide excellent exit signals. Assuming we took the long trade in the above example, we could stay in the trade until the price moved back below the MA, which would signal that the trend might have come to an end. Remember we must run our winning trades as far as possible, so good exit signals are very important.

Because of their popularity and self fulfilling nature, it is worth looking at some particularly common EMA numbers. 10 period, 34 period, and 100 period EMAs are very widely used.

There are some more variations on the simple and exponential moving average formulas we can use. The average can be calculated from prices other than the close price of the bar, for example you might use the high or the low. Another popular variation is to add the high, low, and close prices together and divide by three and then use this when calculating the MA.

The MA calculation can be weighted by the volume associated with a bar instead of giving more weight to just the more recent bars. More volume means more people trading at that price, which means the price is more significant.

In yet another variation, the MA can be plotted in the chart offset from the price. Instead of drawing the average at the point at which it is calculated, it can be plotted a number of bars late. Offsetting can be useful for building trading systems by using two MAs of the same value and offsetting one by several price bars, then using the points where the two cross as buy and sell signals.

Moving average convergence / divergence (MACD) is another way of using two different speed MA's. It plots the difference between the two. Other MA based indicators include channels such as Bollinger bands. These are all different ways of presenting essentially the same information on a chart.

Oscillators

The purpose of all oscillators is to indicate the strength of movement made by the price. They are based on the idea of price having momentum. In the same way a ball thrown into the air has momentum and will gradually slow down and then fall, so a price trend will eventually run out of steam and fall back, even if only briefly.

These types of indicator swing, or oscillate, between high and low values, sometimes fixed, sometimes variable. Very common oscillators include Relative Strength Index (RSI) and Commodity Channel Index (CCI). Let's look at some examples.

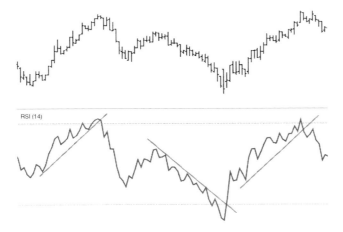

This chart shows a 14 period RSI, which is to say that the last 14 price bars are used in its calculation. The RSI oscillates between values of +100 and 0.

The dashed parallel lines on the RSI portion of the chart, which can be configured as desired, indicate oversold and overbought conditions. The theory is that when the RSI crosses above the upper line, the stock has become overbought and is due to drop or at least go sideways for a breather; in other words, the price is likely to run out of momentum. The opposite applies to the lower line.

There are numerous strategies for trading from the RSI, two common ones are:
- Buy when it crosses above 50, and sell when it crosses below.
- Draw trend lines on the RSI the same way as you would on the price. When the trend line is broken, buy or sell accordingly.

In the above example you can see three trend lines have been drawn on the RSI. Where each line is broken, so the price ends its trend and starts a new trend in the opposite direction.

Here is the same chart, but this time with a 14 period CCI (Commodity Channel Index), an oscillator which moves up and down around a 0 line (the dashed line). The CCI is actually showing you the distance between price and its moving average, it's just another way of displaying that information. When the CCI is at 0, the price is at the moving average.

CCI is often traded in similar ways to RSI. Bounces off or near the 0 line can be traded (this is effectively the price bouncing off its moving average, just plotted differently). Trend line breaks like that shown above also work well. Selling when the CCI turns whilst at extreme values is another strategy, although these overbought and oversold signals are more useful for exiting trades as they show the end of a trend better than the start of a new one.

Other Oscillator Plays

As with MAs, it is entirely possible to overlay two copies of the same oscillator calculated over different periods, and trade crosses. It is also possible to apply a moving average to an oscillator and trade the crosses above and below this MA.

Price patterns, particularly triangles and simple support and resistance lines, work just as well on some oscillators as they do on the price itself. Drawing such lines on these indicators can often be easier than drawing them on the price, because the lines are smoother and the patterns easier to spot.

Divergences between price and an oscillator provide excellent early warnings of a possible change in direction. In the previous chart example, in the two highlighted areas you can see that the price makes a new low but the CCI doesn't follow suit, instead it's rising. This divergence cannot continue, and either the price or CCI must move to resolve it, and most often it is the price which moves to follow the oscillator. The divergence in this example is further confirmed when the zero-line on the CCI is broken. The trend line on the CCI is also broken, giving us three distinct signals that a change of direction is likely.

Summary

Indicators can give us a summary view of price action. They can be traded on their own, but more commonly in conjunction with the price or another indicator as a confirming signal.

Moving average based indicators are lagging in their nature, they tell you what has already happened. Oscillators on the other hand, are sometimes referred to as leading indicators (although they're really not) because they can give prior warning of what the price might do. However, as with all TA, such a warning shouldn't be traded on its own, but only with confirmation from another signal, usually given by the price itself.

As a final word on indicators, beware of *analysis paralysis*! This is an extremely common affliction caused by having too many indicators which end up giving conflicting signals. The trader, faced with too much information to analyse, cannot make a decision and so ends up "paralysed", not taking a trade. Nothing in TA is absolute; it will always be possible to find an indicator that says buy when everything else says sell, if you look hard enough. Remember that as with most things in life, the simplest solution is usually the best. The more obvious a trading signal is, the more people will see it and trade it, and the more chance it has of success.

CHAPTER 8 - PLACING TRADES

"The longer one lives, the more one realises that nothing is a dish for every day."
Norman Douglas

Order Types

We've looked at ways we can make decisions as to when to enter and exit the market (i.e. when to buy and sell), now we must look at ways of actually doing so by executing trades. Trades are made by issuing orders to buy and sell, just like we might place an order in a restaurant. In all markets there are a number of types of buy and sell order that we can use:

- Market
- Limit
- Stop
- Stop-Limit

The types of order available for us to use in each market are dependent on the exchange we are trading through (for exchange traded products), the broker we are routing our order through, and the software we are using. It is important to know which order type to use and when, so let's take a look at each of them in more detail

Market Orders

These are the simplest form of order, an instruction to buy or sell a certain quantity of stock (or futures contracts, options, currency, etc) at the market price, which is to say whatever price the market can give us at the time. In theory, when we issue a market order to buy, the order will be filled at the best ask price, and a market sell order will be filled at the best bid price, as these are the best available prices at that point in time.

However in a fast moving market, by the time we hit the buy or sell button, the order is sent to the broker and then on to the exchange where it is matched with someone who will take the opposite side, the price may have moved against us. This movement is called *slippage*. Of course, the price may move in our favour in that time as well, so slippage can be both positive and negative.

The biggest advantage of market orders is that they will get filled very quickly, and so they are ideal for getting out of a trade at speed.

Limit Orders

Limit orders are orders to buy or sell a certain quantity of shares at a specified price *or better*. A limit order will sit in the market until it is either filled, or we cancel it. A limit order to buy would normally be placed below the current price, and a sell limit would be placed above the current price.

Let's look at an example. The market is currently bid 85.20 / 85.25 ask. We want to buy (go long), and don't want to pay more than the current ask price, so we place a limit order at 85.25. Our order goes into the queue at the exchange. This queue is in price order, then time order based on a first-come-first-served basis. If someone is willing to sell to us at our price (or better) we will be filled. Otherwise, the order will sit in the queue until someone sells to us, or we cancel the order.

Here's another example. The market is currently bid 85.20 / 85.25 ask. We think the price will fall to 85.00 and then go up again, so we want to buy (go long) at 85.00. We place a limit order at 85.00. Our order goes into the queue at the exchange. This queue is in price order, then time order. If the price moves low enough, our order will eventually become the best bid and therefore if someone is willing to sell to us at our price (or better) we will be filled. Otherwise, the order will continue to sit in the queue.

As we can see, a limit order ensures we won't get any slippage, we'll only get filled at the order price or better. On the other hand, it doesn't guarantee we will get filled at all, as the price may never meet the order price. This makes limit orders ideal for entering new trades, but not such a good choice for exiting a trade if we need to do so in a hurry because the price is moving against us. It is usually preferable to accept a few points slippage and be out of a bad trade quickly using a market order than put in a limit order that doesn't get filled, leaving us in a losing position that is getting worse by the second. All exchanges support limit orders. Indeed, it is these orders that make up the market depth we looked at earlier.

Stop Orders

A stop order is an order to buy or sell a certain quantity of shares at a specified price *or worse*. The order will sit in the market until either it is filled, or we cancel it. A stop order to buy would normally be placed above the current price, and a sell stop would be placed below it. Once the stop order price is reached, the stop order becomes a market order.

Like a limit order, a stop order does not guarantee a fill, because the price may never trigger it. Unlike a limit order, it doesn't guarantee a fill price, because it becomes a market order when the price reaches it.

Stop orders are typically used to enter a trade based on the price breaking above or below a technical level (i.e. breaking above or below support or resistance), and to exit a trade based on a price moving a certain distance.

Exits are the most common use, and even if we are planning on exiting a trade at a certain level or based on certain criteria, we should always have a stop order in the market as protection. If we lose our internet connection for example, having a stop order a certain distance from our trade means that our exposure, should the market turn against us, is limited. If the market suddenly changes direction, a stop order again can limit our loss if we are unable to manually exit our trade in good time.

A stop order also forces good trading discipline. If a trade goes against us, it's very easy to not exit because we think *"it might go our way again"*. If we have a stop order in place at the maximum amount we are prepared to lose on the trade, the decision to exit is made for us. Having said that, we should endeavour to always exit the trade ourselves correctly, a stop should be a last resort.

Some examples will make the use of stop orders clearer. Here's an example of using one to enter a trade. The market is currently bid 85.20 / 85.25 ask. We think the price is going to break above 85.30, and so we place a stop buy order at 85.32. As soon as the price hits 85.32, the stop order becomes a market order and will be filled at the best price available. We are now long.

Now here's how we might use a stop order to exit. We enter a long trade (i.e. we buy) at 50.35. We expect the market to rise to around 50.75, but don't want to lose more than about 0.15 on this trade if it goes against us, so we place a stop sell order at 50.20. If the market turns quickly, and hits 50.20, the stop order would become a market order and our position would be sold out.

A sensibly placed stop order offers protection from big losses if things don't work out as expected. It's important to get into the habit of always placing a stop order as soon as you enter any trade. This means you are automatically limiting your losses to a (nearly) fixed amount should you not be able to exit the trade yourself for whatever reason. Unfortunately computers do crash, and internet connections do break. If this happens, your stop order is your insurance policy. Some trading software can be set up to automatically enter a stop order at a specific offset as soon as you enter a new trade. If yours has this facility, I urge you to use it (we'll look more at trading software later on).

Stop orders are often trailed behind the price, to lock-in some profit. Looking back at the last example, if the price rose to 50.60 and we still believed it was going to hit our target of 50.75, we might move (or *trail*) our stop order from 50.20 up to 50.45. This means if the market turns and hits our stop, we would be exiting with a profit of 0.10. Again some trading software can manage this trailing of your stop orders automatically, meaning you have less to think about. In fact, a trailing stop can be used as an exit strategy in itself, in the absence of any technical exit target. By trailing a stop order behind the price we can follow a trend until it reverses a significant amount.

Not all exchanges support stop orders, but most brokers will simulate them for you. They will hold the stop order and then send a market order to the exchange if it is hit.

Regardless of whether an exchange natively supports stop orders or not, they never appear in the market depth, so other traders cannot see them. However, many traders will place their stops in very obvious places, such as just below major support or above major resistance. This is one reason why fakeouts (false breakouts) occur, as the big institutional players try and force the price beyond the support or resistance level in order to take out the stops, before dropping or raising the price back again, giving them cheap stock, and you a loss! Consequently, it is advisable to be careful when choosing where to place a stop order, it might need a bit more room than you first think.

Stop Limit Orders

These are stop orders that become limit orders instead of market orders once the price hits them. With stop limit orders as with regular limit orders, we are not guaranteed a fill, but we are guaranteed a certain price or better if we do get filled. Stop limits can be useful for entering the market on a breakout, but are not advisable as exits for the same reason as limit orders — they may not be filled. Not all exchanges support stop limit orders, but many brokers (and some trading software) will simulate them for you.

Summary

We need to be aware of the different order types available to us, and use the right one at the right time. If in any doubt when exiting a trade, we use a market order, that way we are sure we will get out quickly.

Depending on the capabilities of the software we are using, we can use combinations of orders to manage our trade. For example, we might enter on a limit order, then set a stop order to minimise loss, and another limit order at our target price to get us out automatically when we reach it. Once either the target limit order, or the stop order are filled, the other would be automatically cancelled.

In Part Three when we look at the trading strategy we will be using, we'll see some worked examples of these order types in action.

CHAPTER 9 - TRADING OBJECTIVES REVISITED

"Our greatest glory is not in never falling, but in rising every time we fall."
Confucius

Some Revision

Our objective as day traders is to take consistent daily profits from the market. In order to do that we need to:

- Try and win more trades than we lose, but this is not essential.
- Make sure that our winning trades are bigger on average than our losing trades. This *is* essential!

To achieve our objective, we want to take only good, high probability trades, i.e. trades where we can see we have several things going for us, the more the better. If we are right about the trade, we must try and squeeze as much profit from it as possible, and not just take the money and run as soon as we see some profit on the table. If we are wrong, we must acknowledge the fact and exit the trade with as small a loss as possible.

Again, this last point cannot be overstated; we must exit losing trades quickly. There is no shame in taking a loss, it is as much a part of the job of trading as taking a profit.

Risk To Reward Ratio

A risk to reward ratio is simply the ratio of potential loss if a trade doesn't go the way we expected (risk) to potential profit if it does (reward). There are two ways we can use this ratio to improve our profitability:

- To figure out if a trade is worth taking.
- To figure out where we should exit if the trade doesn't work out.

In both cases we need to know the potential profit (reward) that the possible trade in front of us is offering. It's important to be realistic about the target we have for a trade. We have already looked at some targets provided by patterns like triangles. Other targets we can use include previous areas of support or resistance. The market has memory and if the price couldn't get through a certain level before, it will probably stop there again the next time, even if only temporarily. We'll look more at targets in Part Three, when we look in detail at the strategy we'll be trading.

As well as potential reward, we should also look at where we will exit the trade if we are wrong. Sometimes this will be obvious; perhaps we are entering on a bounce off a support line, in which case we will exit if the price drops below that support, because the bounce hasn't carried through. Other times there will be no obvious exit point.

If we can see a clear exit point that we'll use should the trade not work out, then we can see what our maximum risk is, and we can calculate the risk to reward ratio for the trade, and thus decide if the trade is worth risking our money on. For example, let's imagine we are looking at a chart for RIM stock. The last price is currently 35.02. According to our analysis, we believe there is a good probability that the price is going to rise, and we can see an exit target of a strong resistance line at 35.50. So the potential reward is 48 cents per share held, assuming we were able to enter at the current price. The reason we think the price will rise is because it has just bounced off a strong support line at 35.00. Allowing for wiggle room, we know that if the price dropped to 34.95, the trade would not have worked out (because the bounce hasn't followed through). So our maximum loss, assuming we could exit at that price without slippage, would be 7 cents. The risk to reward ratio to this trade is 1:6 to 8 (7 cents risk to 48 cents reward). This is a good ratio, so the trade is well worth the risk.

In many cases we don't know what the maximum risk is. The risk reward ratio can still help us out though, by telling us where we should exit if the trade doesn't go our way. Here's another example. This time we are looking at Amazon.com stock. The price is at 185.45 and we think it's going higher. We have an exit target of 186.00, so our potential reward is 55 cents per share. There's no obvious place to exit if the trade doesn't go well, so we use risk:reward as a way of calculating one. We have decided that the maximum risk to reward ratio we are comfortable with is 1 to 4. In other words, four times potential profit to potential loss. So we don't want to lose more than a quarter of the potential profit this trade is offering, i.e. one quarter of 55 cents, or 13 cents (rounded down). Our risk:reward ratio is telling us that if the trade moves 13 cents against us, we must exit.

The actual risk reward ratio we decide to use in this way will depend on the trading strategy we're using, and the percentage of winning trades versus losing trades it typically throws up, as well as our money management profile. What's that you might ask? Let's find out!

Money Management

Careful money management is one of the keys to successful trading. The purpose of a money management strategy is to ensure we preserve our capital to keep us in the game even when we are not winning trades. We do this by never risking more than a certain amount of our capital on any single trade, and by never allowing ourselves to lose more than a certain amount of money in any one day, week, or month.

As we have already seen, losing trades are part of the business of trading, and are to be expected. But we must control those losses so that when we suffer a string of them, which according to the laws of probability is inevitable, we do not wipe out our account.

Our maximum risk should be large enough to ensure that we can take trades with good profit potential, but not so large as to cause us serious financial damage if we consistently lose.

Let's work through an example. We'll assume we are starting out full time day trading, with no prior experience. We have a starting balance of $15,000 to trade with. We are prepared to give ourselves six months in which to become profitable. In such a scenario, we could have a strategy whereby we risk a maximum loss of $200 a day. If we hit this limit, we would stop trading for the rest of the day. If we hit the limit four days running, we would take the fifth day off, meaning we had lost a maximum of $800 for the week.

If we were to have a really bad run, and lost three weeks straight, we would take the fourth week off, giving us a maximum loss of $2,400 for the month. If we lost the maximum we have permitted ourselves every month, we would be down $14,400 at the end of our six month limit. Our plan would have allowed us the full six months, without wiping out the account.

Taking this a step further, if we are allowing ourselves to lose up to $200 a day, we know that we cannot possibly risk more than $200 on any single trade. Depending on our trading strategy, a realistic risk might be $100 per trade. So if we saw a trade with a good risk : reward ratio and high probability, but the maximum loss if the trade went wrong was more than $100, we would pass on that trade.

By sticking to our money management strategy we are ensuring we can stay in the game for at least a certain amount of time, and have ample opportunity to take at least a certain number of trades each day. To lose every day for six months would be a major achievement in any case! And as we'll see later on in this book, we will take further steps to make sure that simply doesn't happen.

Knowing in advance how much you can possibly lose in any one trade and in any one day takes much of the psychological pressure off trading. Psychology is a big part of trading, and something that will be covered in chapter 12.

CHAPTER 10 - PUTTING IT ALL TOGETHER

"Example is the best precept."
Aesop

A Worked Trade Example

Let's now take an example to put together some of the concepts we have covered, and see how we can actually use this knowledge to make some money from the stock market. For this example we will assume we have a starting account balance of $10,000. We are watching a fictitious NASDAQ stock.

Chart 1:

When looking at any chart, we want to first determine where any support and resistance can be found. The horizontal line has been used to mark resistance that occurred around at the areas labelled 1 and 2. The vertical line delineates the start of the next trading session (i.e. the start of the day). The first thing to notice is that the price starts off the new trading session in a strong up-trend. When it retraces, it bounces off the earlier resistance line. So resistance has become support. This is an important line on the chart.

Chart 2:

As the chart unfolds we can add in some more lines. The lower trend line clearly shows us the overall up-trend. We also now have some resistance at the *High Of Day* (HOD), which has been marked here. By connecting three low points in price, we can draw in another smaller up-trend line. Now we can see that we have an ascending triangle forming on this chart.

This means we have our first possible trading opportunity. If the price breaks out of the top of the triangle, we know that there is a good probability it will continue the up-trend.

We must now assess the risk and reward of this potential trade. We know that when a triangle pattern breaks out, the price will often travel for the same distance as it covered at the widest point of the pattern. If we use the earlier support / resistance line at approximately $54.05 as the confirmed start of the triangle, and subtract that from the price at the top of the pattern ($54.55) then we can see that this distance is 50 cents. Thus we can reasonably hope that if the price breaks out of the top, it will continue on to $54.55 + $0.50, i.e. $55.05. The potential reward for this trade is 50 cents per share.

To work out the risk we must calculate how much we would lose on the trade if the price didn't do as we expected. If the price broke through the top of the triangle, then came back down and fell below the up-trend (green) line, then we would know the pattern had failed. So we can see in the chart above that if the price got to $54.40 we would know the trade was not working. Given that a breakout of the triangle would have us buying this share at a price of about $54.55 - $54.60, if we were to have to sell it at $54.50 then our loss would be 20 cents per share. So the risk on this trade is 20 cents.

The risk:reward is $0.20 : $0.50, or a ratio of 1 to 2.5. Given that we are looking for a minimum of 1 to 2 (i.e. a potential reward of at least double the potential loss), this trade is acceptable to us. Now we must wait and see if the triangle pattern breaks out.

Chart 3:

Chart 3 shows that the price has indeed broken out. We could have used a market order to buy this stock at the time it broke through the top of the triangle. If the price was moving quickly, there may have been a difference in the price our order was filled at and the price we were seeing on the screen at the time, so called slippage.

In this example, we will assume we purchased 500 shares and the price paid was $54.60. The total cost is 500 x $54.60 = $27,300. Our broker allows us 4:1 margin, so the margin requirement is a quarter of the total cost, i.e $6,825. The broker allocates this margin from our account, leaving us an available balance of $3,175.

Now we are long 500 shares, the most important thing we must do is place a stop order to exit our position if the price goes against us. Remember a stop order is an order to sell at a certain price or worse. We know that if the price hits $54.40 the pattern has failed and we want to exit, so we can place a stop sell order for 500 shares at $54.40. With the stop order in place, it doesn't matter if we lose our internet connection, or our PC blows up, if the price goes against us the order will trigger and close our position, limiting our loss.

Chart 4:

As the chart continues, we see that the breakout has followed through nicely. The price retraced after the initial break, and bounced off the existing (long) up-trend line. At this point we could move our stop order up to just below the trend line, which is now at our initial entry price of $54.60. This means if the price then starts to go back down, our stop order would sell our stock for the same price we paid for it and we would not make a loss (ignoring the brokerage commission charges). The trade is now effectively risk free.

Our target price was the top of the triangle pattern ($54.55) plus the triangle target (50 cents), i.e. $55.05. As we can see, the price slightly exceeded the target and then fell back. We could have chosen to close out our trade at the target by selling with a market order.

Alternatively we could have put in a limit sell order at the target price. Remember a limit order is an order to trade at a specified price or better, so a limit sell order at $55.05 would have sold at that price or higher, assuming it got there.

Yet another alternative, because the up-trend was quite strong, would have been to have held on to our stock and waited for the trend line to fail. The price broke through the trend line at $55.00 so selling our stock here would have resulted in a slightly smaller profit, but had the line held as support then we might have realised a larger one than simply selling at the initial target.

Assuming we sold our stock at the target price of $56.05, we would have realised a profit of $0.45 per share. We traded 500 shares, so our profit on this trade was 500 x $0.45 = $225. The trade lasted about an hour, so that's not bad for an hour's work!

Chapter 11 - Setting Up To Trade

"It's probably true that hard work never killed anyone, but I figure why take the chance?"
Ronald Reagan

Equipment

As with most professions, there are certain tools we need to day trade. First, a computer, and the faster the better. More RAM (memory) will help more than a faster processor. Either a Mac or PC can be used, but bear in mind that the great majority of trading software runs under Windows, so if you use a Mac, you will really need Windows running on it as well. That can be done using BootCamp, Parallels, Virtual Box or something similar.

Multiple monitors might look good in films, but in reality they are not necessary. As we'll see in Part Three, a single screen makes life much easier.

Desktops or laptops can be used, and indeed there are some advantages to trading from a laptop which we'll look at in just a second. Tablets like iPads aren't recommended as there isn't the breadth of specialist software for them, and they're not good at running two things at once. As we will see in a moment, we will normally be running charts and broker software simultaneously.

Your computer will of course need an internet connection so that it can talk to the outside world — the brokers and exchanges. It doesn't need to be super fast, but it does need good response times because we don't want to be viewing price information that is a few seconds old. A lot can happen in a few seconds. Therefore satellite connections are not advisable because of the time lag they introduce. Broadband (xDSL) connections are now cheap and readily available in almost all areas, so it would be a false economy to try and trade with anything less than a 2Mbit/s connection.

If you're serious about making a living from trading, then some form of backup internet connection is advisable, perhaps another ISP, or a cellular connection (3G and 4G dongles are cheap and easy to come by). If your ISP has problems, you don't want to be stuck in a trade you cannot exit. A slower connection will be fine as a backup, it just needs to be good enough to connect to your broker so you can close any open orders.

An Uninterruptible Power Supply (UPS) is also a useful addition to the trader's set-up. If the power fails a UPS can keep the computer on long enough to exit any open trades. If you trade from a laptop computer (as I do) then you effectively have a UPS already: the battery! Another advantage of using a laptop is you can trade from anywhere. Remember though that if your modem or router requires mains power, you'll lose your internet connection during a power cut.

Software

There are two types of software that we need:

1. A charting package. This takes the price data provided from the exchange and turns it into the charts we trade from. Some examples include eSignal, Sierra Chart, and QuoteTracker. These vary in price from free to a few hundred dollars a month. Even if the software is free, you will need to pay for price data from the exchange. The cost of these price feeds is fixed by the exchange, although you wont get your data directly from them, it will come through a third party. This might be the same company that supplies your software (as is the case with eSignal for example), or you could choose to go with a different supplier if your software supplier doesn't have a price feed available.

2. Order entry software. This is normally supplied by your broker, and is used to actually place your orders and manage your trades.

Some brokers will supply both charting and order entry software, and some charting software can be used for order entry.

Brokers

We also need an account with a broker. There are a couple of possibilities here: a traditional broker, who is a member of the exchange we want to trade on, and who will charge us a commission fee for handling our orders, or a Spread Bet or CFD company.

As a reminder, Spread Bet and CFD companies sell their own products which are based on the underlying exchange-traded product. If we trade with them, we must do so at their prices. We cannot put our own limit order into the market and wait and see if somebody somewhere in the world takes it.

Examples of real brokers (note that these are not recommendations, just examples) include http://www.interactivebrokers.com and http://www.tradestation.com

Examples of spread betting and CFD companies (again, these are not recommendations, purely examples) are http://www.cmcmarkets.com and http://www.etrade.com

Personal Choice

Choosing a broker and charting program is a bit like choosing a car. They all do much the same thing, so the choice really comes down to individual circumstances and personal preferences. For example, you may prefer a broker who has an office in your country, or one who offers telephone backup if the internet stops working.

It's well worth ringing round a few brokers and talking to them about the way they work. As you talk to them, ask yourself, is this someone you can work with?

Do the same with charting software. All the popular packages have free trial versions, so give them a go and see what you think. You wouldn't buy a car without a test drive, so why choose charts or a broker without test driving them first?

Costs

There are numerous costs associated with trading, not all of which you necessarily need to pay immediately. The computer and internet connection you probably already have, so these are unlikely to be a major outlay.

Charting software is normally paid for on a fixed term license fee or rolling month basis. Some charting programs are actually free, although bear in mind you wont get the same level of technical support from free software.

As mentioned, exchanges charge a fee for providing their price data to you. These fees are passed on by both the broker and the charting software company. They vary from exchange to exchange, and product set to product set.

Commission charges are your variable cost. Your broker will charge a commission for handling your order. The exchange also charges commission, but this is included in that charged by the broker. Fees vary widely, and are not always related to the quality of service. Some brokers will also charge a standing fee for managing your account.

If you are holding margined trades open overnight, you may be charged interest on the margin as it is effectively a loan from the broker. On the other hand, cash balances (including those resulting from holding a short position) will attract interest from the broker, although of course this will be at a lower rate.

It should be pointed out that Spread Bet / CFD companies will not charge any exchange data fees because you are seeing their own prices. Some companies also do not charge commission on your trades, although in reality you are paying for your trading through an increased bid / ask spread.

This might sound like a lot of things to pay for, but relative to the costs of embarking on almost any other kind of business venture, the costs to start trading are negligible. Aside from a computer, the biggest fixed cost is the software and data feeds. As these are paid for monthly, they can easily be budgeted for, and paid from profits.

Chapter 12 - Trader Psychology

"If you can't control your emotions, being in the market is like walking into a heated area wearing a backpack full of explosives."
Charles Ellis

The 80/20 Rule

Trading is 20% about reading the market and knowing what to do based on your trading strategy, and 80% about actually doing the right thing at the right time. Psychological factors are one of the most overlooked areas of trading. The reason most traders fail is not because they cannot read the market, but because they do not manage themselves properly. They fail because of:

Ego - After a winning streak it is easy to become complacent and take your eye off the ball. The market eats egos for breakfast!

Fear - Fear that a winning trade might turn into a losing one causes traders to exit early and not maximise their profit. Fear of taking a loss when a trade doesn't go as planned makes many traders watch the loss grow bigger and bigger as they desperately *hope* the price will turn round again. As those losses mount up, traders then start to experience fear of actually "pulling the trigger" and entering the next trade. They constantly ask themselves *"what if it doesn't work?"*

Greed - After a trade has hit its target, greed can lead a trader to stay with it as they hope for even more profit. Greed also leads to over trading, entering sub-standard trades in the vain hope of more profit.

Lack of self control and discipline - Not sticking to the trading strategy means that traders will take sub-standard trades, trades that either don't show clear entry criteria or that don't fit the risk : reward profile. Traders may continue trading after they have hit their loss limit in the hope that *"this one is going to win it all back"*. Trading without self control is simply gambling, and gamblers always lose in the end.

Lack of patience - Again, it's all too easy to become impatient waiting for a good high probability low risk trade to come along, and to enter on some sub-standard reason.

So trading psychology is all about managing ego, fear, greed, and hope. Traders must develop an abundance of discipline, self control, and patience in order to succeed in the long term.

Execution Is Everything

A winning trader plans the trade, then trades the plan. Once you have decided on your trade, you must remain emotionally detached and concentrate on executing it to the best of your ability. To help maintain that detachment, it helps to remember that you have no control whatsoever over the market. If it goes against you there is nothing you can do about it. There is no point in becoming angry or despondent, doing so will only lead to loss. However, you do have total control over your trade. Direct your attention to trading according to plan, then it doesn't matter if the trade is a winner or a loser, you can give yourself a pat on the back for executing it correctly.

Over time, as long as you continue to execute trades correctly, the winners will add up and you will be profitable. But never take your eye off the ball, don't become complacent because as soon as you do you will start taking unnecessary risks or become greedy, and will soon lose.

The importance of psychology is something that only becomes truly apparent once one starts trading with real money and experiencing the emotions for themselves.

Emotional Detachment

Remaining detached from your trading is easier said than done, but there are things you can do to help. Firstly, never think in terms of money when trading. Think in terms of points won or lost. This has even more benefit as you build up your position and start trading in larger sizes (more shares per trade).If you look at a trade in terms of points, it will carry the same emotional and psychological weight whether your trade size makes a point worth $1, $10, or even $100.

Commentary Technique

If you find yourself becoming emotionally involved in a trade, try giving a running commentary on it. Talking out loud occupies the mind, and therefore it doesn't have time to start thinking about fear or greed. Talking through your trade will also focus your attention on the execution — is the trade still valid? Should you be moving your stop? How much further has it got to run? It sounds simple, and it is, but this is a very effective way of keeping disciplined.

When using this technique it's important to actually talk out loud. Physical speech uses a different portion of the brain to just thinking about your trade. It can have an amazing effect.

An extension of this method is to use an imaginary trading coach. If you talk through your thought process on every trade as if explaining it to someone far more experienced than yourself, you are more likely to do the right thing. You wouldn't enter a low probability trade if the world's greatest trader was looking over your shoulder, so why do it on your own? Again, talk out loud as if to someone sitting right beside you, it will make a big difference.

Handling Fear (And Hope, And Greed)

There will still be many times while you are trading that fears start to enter your mind. Many of those have been mentioned earlier, such as the fear of a trade becoming a loss, or a profit target not being hit. Fear, and other intense emotions, can make us do irrational things, and when trading that usually means things which are not part of our trading strategy.

Fears are best dealt with at a time when we have a clear and detached mind, i.e. when we are not trading. A highly effective method for dealing with these emotional barriers is to write them down as you experience them while trading, and then deal with them later when you are not trading.

Let's take an example. You are in a trade which has started to show a profit, and you become tempted to take that profit now instead of letting the trade run on to its logical target. Perhaps your previous trade was a losing one and the profit shown by this trade is enough to cover that loss. Such a temptation is understandable, and can be exceptionally strong. However, exiting a trade just to cover a loss is hardly likely to make profits over the long term, and is the wrong thing to do. Write down your temptation, and why you feel you want to do what you want to do.

Later on when you are not trading and consequently are emotionally detached from the market, go back and look at what you have written. Consider your trading strategy, and then write your own rational response to that fear. For example, you might write *"Taking a profit early will mean that I will never experience big winning trades and will therefore lose money in the long run"*.

Next time you experience the same feeling when you are trading, you can go back and read your own rational reasons as to why you should not follow your temptation. However, you will be surprised to find that more often than not, simply going through this process of writing down your emotions and confronting them after the market has closed will in itself banish the fears and stop them cropping up while trading.

Over Trading

A common affliction among new traders is over trading. The desire to make money means that the trader finds themselves taking as many trades as possible, and inevitably that means they end up entering substandard trades.

I often see new traders making ten, fifteen, sometimes even twenty or more trades each day. I rarely take more than six or seven in a day, usually fewer. We're looking for quality, not quantity. We want to select only the finest trade setups, those which offer the greatest probability of following through, the highest profit potential, and the lowest risk. Taking unnecessary trades adds to the workload, erodes confidence, and eats away at profits.

The single best way of combatting over trading is to artificially limit the number of trades you can take each day. Start with a limit of one. Once you have taken a single trade and exited, switch off your computer and walk away. Don't allow yourself to look at another chart for the rest of the day. Get into the habit of doing this, and you will quickly find yourself becoming much more choosey about the one trade you can take. When you know you only have one shot, you are going to make sure it's a good one.

When you feel comfortable doing so (when you are consistently selecting a good trade for your one shot per day), raise your limit to two trades. And then three, four, and five, Eventually you can remove the limit, after all, some days there will be an abundance of amazing opportunities to be traded and you don't want to miss out when those days happen. But if ever you find yourself slipping back into over trading, immediately reimpose your trade limit to bring yourself back in line.

Trigger Trouble (Problems Entering)

The next most common issue I see new traders face is that they will be sat in front of an excellent trade setup, with everything on the chart shouting "buy!" They know that they should enter the trade, but fear prevents them from pulling the trigger and actually hitting the buy button.

There's no simple cure for this problem, ultimately it comes down to a lack of confidence in the strategy, the traders own ability, or both. Confidence comes from experience, so this is a chicken-and-egg situation. To gain the confidence to enter trades effortlessly, you need experience of entering trades!

Fortunately, we can get this experience in a risk-free way through simulated trading. This is something we'll look at in more detail in Part Three. Suffice it to say, by gaining experience in a risk free way, we can gain confidence both that the strategy we are trading really does work, and in our own ability to follow it. That confidence translates directly into an ability to execute trades efficiently and ruthlessly.

Exit Issues

Getting into a trade is half the battle. The other half is getting out at the right time. Exit too early and you are missing out on profits. Exit too late and you risk losing profits that should already be in the bank, as the price retraces. And that's just on profitable trades. Exiting from a losing trade can be even harder. Exiting at a loss means admitting that your opinion of the price direction was wrong, and that can be hard to do. It's in our nature to dislike admitting that we are wrong about anything.

As with entering, the ability to ruthlessly exit a trade when the strategy says is the right time, instead of when we feel like it, comes down to having total confidence that the strategy works. Sometimes the strategy might not extract the maximum available profit from the trade, but that's normal and to be expected. No strategy is clairvoyant and so no strategy can always take all the money that's on the table. As long as on average it wins more than it loses, your strategy is going to make you money. But only if you execute it properly. So once again, exit problems can be solved by building confidence in your strategy, which you do by gaining experience.

Summary

It is important to use all of these techniques when trading, and to use them all the time. It is easy to have a good run of winners and think that you have conquered your emotions and are now a successful winning trader. Thinking like that leads to complacency, sub-standard trading, and very quickly to loss.

By the same token a run of losing trades can lead one to feel that they are a failure, that they cannot trade.

Try at all times to remain detached, not to feel elated at winning trades and despondent at losses, and you will avoid the destructive emotional roller coaster that is the downfall of many a trader.

PART TWO - BASIC EXERCISES

Introduction

The exercises on the following pages will give you an opportunity to try analysing support, resistance, and trends, as well as basic chart patterns. After each chart segment and question set, the chart is repeated with some analysis added to it and an explanation of the patterns.

You should complete these exercises before moving on to Part Three. If your answers differ from those given, or you find you can't answer some of the questions, you should go back and study the relevant section in Part One before continuing.

Exercise 1 Questions

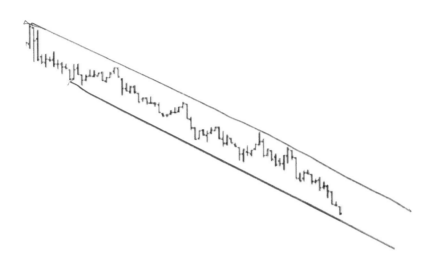

1. What overall pattern is shown here?

2. Can you draw any meaningful lines on this chart to highlight the pattern?

3. Can you see any flags?

NO flags

Exercise 1 Answers

1. The overall basic pattern here is a down-trend. Clearly the price is making a series of lower highs and lower lows. In such a trend we would be favouring short trades, in other words we would be looking for low risk opportunities to sell stock we didn't own in anticipation of buying it back at a lower price to make a profit.

2. The trend line has been drawn in on the chart above.

3. There are numerous flags in this down-trend, two of the most obvious ones have been marked with the short lines. These flags give ideal entry signals. When the price fails to break through the downtrend line (bounces) and then breaks through the bottom of the flag pattern, there is a high probability it will continue downwards. This one chart example shows at least four places where the price bounced off the down trend line giving trading high probability opportunities.

Exercise 2 Questions

1. Can you find any support and / or resistance lines on this chart?

2. What happens to the support or resistance later?   BreAKS

Exercise 2 Answers

1. The two main support and resistance lines are marked here.

2. The upper line starts out as resistance, the price cannot break through it and keeps bouncing off. Later on, after the price has bounced from the lower support line, it finally breaks through the resistance and continues higher.

Later still, when the price comes back to the previous resistance line, it bounces off that, thus old resistance has become new support.

Also of note on this chart is that after breaking through the resistance line, one price bar spiked back below it. From this chart alone, there is no way of knowing if this spike was caused by a single trade that occurred away from the real market price, or if lots of activity caused the price to trade lower then return and continue upwards.

Exercise 3 Questions

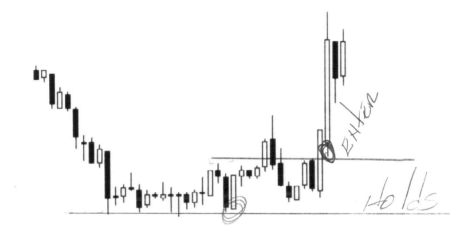

1. Can you find any support and / or resistance on this chart?

2. How might you have traded from this pattern?

Exercise 3 Answers

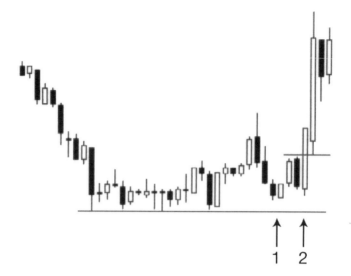

1. There is a solid support line that has formed at the bottom of the chart.

2. Having repeatedly failed to break through the support line, the price eventually makes a higher low (labelled here as 1). This tells us that the sellers are losing control, more buyers are coming into the market stopping the price from falling any lower. When the price makes a second higher low (labelled 2), the market is telling us that it's starting to move higher; a new up-trend could be forming.

A possible entry would be to enter on a break of the previous high, shown here by the short horizontal line. Notice that as in the earlier exercise, this previous high once broken becomes new support as the price actually comes down and bounces from it.

This is a higher risk trade than the flag patterns in Exercise 1, because we are now trading the start of what we think is a new trend instead of a well established trend. However, the risk is clearly defined. We could place our stop order below the previous low, or just under the major (red) support line. The reward is also potentially higher because we are getting in near the beginning of a new trend instead of some way along it when it may be coming to an end. We are balancing higher risk against higher potential reward.

Exercise 4 Questions

1. What patterns do you see here?

2. What lines could you draw on this chart?

3. How might you trade this pattern?

Exercise 4 Answers

1. There are actually two patterns here, the up-trend, and a rectangle.

2. The up-trend is shown, and the support and resistance lines that form the rectangle are also marked.

3. Because the price is moving in an up-trend, we would be looking for an entry into a long trade as giving the lowest risk, in other words we would be looking to buy in anticipation of selling at a higher price for a profit.

When the price enters the rectangle consolidation pattern, we know that any breakout to the upside is a good opportunity and that the price has good probability of moving at least the same distance as the height of the rectangle. The price breaks out to the upside, and at the same time is bouncing off the up-trend line giving us two signals in our favour. We could buy at this breakout and put our stop order in just below the trend line. As the price continues to rise, we can trail the stop just below the trend line thus locking in our profit as the price increases.

Exercise 5 Questions

1. What patterns can you see on this chart? *Pullback*

2. Draw on any lines you think might be useful.

3. If you wanted to go long on this stock, where would be a good entry?

Exercise 5 Answers

1. There are three main patterns on this chart:

- A well established down-trend
- A double bottom
- A new up-trend

2. The diagonal lines mark the trends, and the double bottom is shown by the arrows. The higher low of the double bottom is the indication that the down-trend has ended. However, at this point we don't know if the price is going to start a new up-trend or just consolidate sideways. To confirm an entry we are looking for a breakout over the previous high.

3. The upper of the two horizontal lines shows a safe entry because it breaks a well defined high. The lower line is a possible — more aggressive — entry because it breaks a less well defined high in the price. However, by drawing in what we believe may be a new up-trend line (the second diagonal line), we have clearly defined risk, so the lower horizontal line is actually a lower risk trade as it is nearer to where we would place our stop.

The important point here is that there is no 100% right or wrong way to analyse a chart. Our job as traders is to evaluate risk, reward, and probability, and take entries based on our own money management and risk profile.

Exercise 6 Questions

1. Can you find a pattern in the first half of this chart?

2. If you wanted to enter a new trade, where would you do so, and in what direction?

3. Where would you place your stop?

4. How far might you expect the price to go?

Exercise 6 Answers

1. The pattern is a descending triangle in a down-trend.

2. Because the triangle is descending, and the price trend is downwards, the highest probability trade is a short trade, i.e. selling stock in anticipation of buying it back at a lower price for a profit. Remember though, we would not enter the trade until the price actually breaks out of the triangle pattern.

3. A logical place to put a stop order to exit the trade if it went against us, would be just above the down trend line that marks the top of the triangle. If we wanted a tighter stop (smaller potential loss), we could place it just above the horizontal line that marks the bottom of the triangle.

On many occasions a triangle pattern will break out and the price may then briefly retrace back inside the pattern before continuing in the direction of the break. So we must decide if we are willing to take the risk of that happening and having a smaller loss if the tighter stop is hit, against having a bigger potential loss but less chance of the stop being hit if we use the upper line to place the stop order.

4. The widest point of the triangle gives an approximate price target for any breakout. Here the marker shows that the difference in price at the widest point is approximately 0.40. If we entered short at a price of 33.50, we could reasonably expect the price to go as low as 33.10, and indeed as you can see it met and slightly exceeded this target.

Summary

Reading charts and recognising patterns takes practice. The more charts you look at, the easier it will be to see what is going on. Sometimes you will see nothing going on at all because the price is just going sideways, and recognising that is just as important as seeing the patterns shown here.

There are lots of sources of free stock charts on the internet. Your ongoing action should be to regularly look at as many charts as you can, and analyse them for trends, support, resistance, and patterns.

If you have access to a printer, try printing charts out and drawing lines on them, it will help you enormously in understanding price action.

Finally, remember there is never any 100% right or wrong way to look at a chart. All you can ever do is weigh up probability, risk, and reward. Sometimes very strong patterns will form but then fail for no apparent reason. Your analysis must cater for all outcomes and give you sensible places to exit a trade in such situations

PART THREE - THE TRADING STRATEGY

In this part of the book we are going to look in detail at a day trading strategy that is well proven and can provide consistent daily profits. In other words, a strategy that meets our original objective.

To build the strategy we need to select the market and instrument type we are going to trade, define the type of trades we will be looking for and the sort of risks we are willing to take, and the rewards we expect in return.

We'll look in detail at how we plan our trading session, right through to how we find and execute individual trades.

Too many traders fail because they believe that day trading is difficult, that there must be some holy grail trading system that wins every time, and that this system must be very complicated indeed which is why (they tell themselves) they haven't found it yet.

This is of course, complete nonsense. There is no holy grail in trading. The key to being successful is to keep trading as simple as possible and to stick to defined rules. The simpler and better defined the rules, the easier it is to adhere to them. The trading patterns covered in this course may surprise you in their simplicity; this is the key to their success. So let's get started!

Trading Instruments Review

Before choosing a market to trade, we will briefly review the most popular trading instruments that we learned about in Part One, looking at the advantages and disadvantages of each.

Currencies (Forex)

Advantages: The currency market is the largest market traded in the world . Every day the value of currency transactions exceeds all other markets combined. This means there is no shortage of liquidity, so there is always someone to take the other side of our trade.

Currencies tend to trend more often, for longer, and more consistently than other markets. These trends mean there are usually plenty of entry opportunities.

High gearing (margin) allows us good profit potential from a relatively small starting capital base. Forex usually trades on a margin of 20:1 or higher.

Forex is a 24 hour market which means we can trade at almost any time to suit us.

Generally speaking, brokerage fees are low, and there's usually a free price feed and free charting application with the account.

Finally, there are no restrictions on how often we trade.

Disadvantages: There are a limited number of currency pairs we can usefully trade. If none of them happen to be setting up for potential trades within our trading window (the period of time we are watching the market and able to trade), then we may find nothing to trade on a given day.

Forex is not traded through an exchange, rather through currency brokers, which means the broker sets the prices. This means that the currency market is not entirely transparent.

The 24 hour market can also be a disadvantage. Once in a trade it may be necessary to manage it for a considerable time to get the most out of it. We could become a slave to the market, stuck in front of a screen managing a trade that takes forever. Forex is also relatively slow moving, it may take hours or even days for a move to complete.

The high margin (or leverage) used trading forex is a double edged sword. It means we can ramp up large profits from a small account, but on the other hand it also offers us the potential to make significant losses from a minor investment.

Futures

Advantages: There are a wide variety of futures contracts available to trade through various exchanges around the world, so we can probably find a contract that trades in a time zone to suit us.

Quite high gearing (margin) allows for good profit potential with relatively low startup capital. Brokerage fees and exchange data fees are low, which also lowers the financial barriers to entry.

Futures can be fast moving allowing us to make our daily profit in a short space of time.

There are a good selection of brokers and software available and there are no restrictions on the number of times we can trade.

Disadvantages: Realistically, because of considerations of liquidity, there are fewer contracts available to trade than a cursory glance may suggest. Some types of contract must also be discounted because they are seasonal, such as grains or animal products.

Because different contracts have their own "personality", it becomes necessary to specialise in just one or two, and get to know them well, to learn how they move.

The contracts we would be interested in trading are largely unpredictable in terms of when during the trading session they will offer good trades. So it is necessary to watch them for the entire duration of the session, with no guarantee that a high quality trade will present itself.

Although quick, moves are relatively small and so to get the best from them requires highly skilled entries and exits. In short, futures contracts can be difficult to trade profitably.

The smallest tradable quantity is a single contract, which due to gearing is high value, so it becomes difficult to limit our risk.

Stocks

Advantages: There is huge availability. There are stock markets all around the world, and the larger stock markets have all the liquidity we could want.

There is a good selection of brokers and software available for stock traders, and broker and exchange data fees are low. Most markets are now fully electronic with automatic order matching, and so are completely transparent.

There are many thousands of individual stocks available to trade, so we can go looking for stocks that are giving trading opportunities rather than waiting for trading opportunities to come to us.

There is lots of scalability in terms of how much risk we take because we can trade very small quantities, in theory from a single share (some brokers have minimum size) and we can scale up to thousands per trade if we want.

Stocks in some markets move very fast indeed, giving the chance for quick profits. They make sizeable moves which are more forgiving of poor entries and exits. That means stocks are easier to trade profitably.

In some markets, moves occur at predictable times of the day, so we can tune our trading window to get the best out of the market in a small space of time.

Individual stocks within the same market usually exhibit the same characteristics in terms of the way they move, so unlike futures it is not necessary to become familiar with each one.

Disadvantages: Lower gearing (less generous margin) than other instruments means we need more capital to make equivalent profits with stocks as, say, futures.

Some markets (notably the US) place restrictions on how often we can trade . We will look more at this later on.

Instruments Summary

With their numerous advantages and limited downside, stocks give us an excellent opportunity to find regular profitable low risk high probability trades every day. The fact we can build up from a very small position size when we first start trading gives them added appeal.

The first part of our strategy is decided then. We are going to trade stocks. Now we need to look at which stock market to trade.

World Stock Markets

Europe: European stocks tend to be very slow moving, which does not make them ideal for day trading where we want quick moves that can give us our profits in a short timeframe. Buying stocks in the UK is very expensive. Broker fees are high, and we must also pay stamp duty on every transaction. Other European markets are similarly expensive.

Asia & Australia: These markets can be discounted by most readers of this book due to obvious problems with time zones. They also exhibit many of the limitations of the European markets in that they tend to be slower moving, and more expensive to trade. That said, readers of prior editions of this book tell me they have adapted the strategies described within to work in European, Australian, and Indian markets, with some good success.

United States of America: This is the market we are going to build a trading strategy on, and here is why: it's huge. There are thousands of stocks available. It also has massive liquidity. We need to have lots of people trading the same market because when we want to get in or out of a trade, there needs to be someone to take the other side. When we buy, someone has to sell to us. The more players there are, the more liquidity, so the easier it is to enter and exit trades at the price we want. This becomes more important as we increase the size of our positions (the number of shares we buy and sell in one go). The US market also has huge volume. There is no point in having lots of players in the market if they only trade tiny quantities and we want to trade big size.

The US market is fast. Moves can happen very quickly, meaning we can earn our daily profit in a small amount of time. Less work and more money. It's also predictable. Moves tend to happen at the same times of the day. That means we can plan our trading accordingly, concentrating just on the periods of time when trades are likely to occur, instead of watching a screen all day hoping for something to turn up.

US stocks are generally priced much higher than European ones. This is important because it means moves are bigger, giving more profit potential. For example, a typical UK stock might be priced at £12.00. If this stock moves 5% in the course of the day (which would be considered a large move), that is a total of 60 pence. It's unlikely that the entire move would occur in one go, but even if half of it did, that would be a 30 pence move. If we capture two thirds of the move we will net 20 pence per share traded (about 30 US cents).

US stocks on the other hand, are typically priced in the range $20 - $100. A 5% move on a $50.00 stock is $2.50, and if half of that move occurs in one go ($1.25) and we get two thirds of that, we will net around 83 cents per share we trade. In reality, US stocks tend to move further during the day than European ones anyway, increasing profit potential even more. If we think back to the example of IBM right at the start of this book, the price moved a huge amount during the day, even though at the time it closed its actual gain was negligible.

A final point in favour of US stocks is the costs of trading (brokerage and data fees) are very low.

Market Specifics

Having decided to trade US stocks, let's turn our attention to the stock exchanges we'll be trading. There are a few in operation, and two in particular that are of interest to us.

NASDAQ

NASDAQ is an acronym which stands for The National Association of Securities Dealers Automated Quotation system. It is the highest volume stock exchange in the US, accounting for more than 50% of all US trade volume. In fact trading volume regularly exceeds two and a half billion shares bought and sold on the NASDAQ every day. Its fully electronic trade matching means very fast fills and total transparency. It is a level playing field. If you place an order to buy 100 shares 0.1 seconds ahead of an institution who places and order to buy 100,000 shares, your order takes priority and gets filled first.

NASDAQ's Level 2 market depth facility gives much more information than any similar service (although for our strategy we don't need to use this).

Generally speaking the NASDAQ leans towards technology and new media stocks, and there are more than 3,200 companies listed on the exchange. This exchange is widely used by day traders, which is one reason it offers excellent liquidity.

NYSE

NYSE stands for the New York Stock Exchange, the older of the two primary American exchanges. The NYSE offers a huge range of stocks to trade. It has massive daily volume and high liquidity. Although not quite as high as the NASDAQ, it still regularly exceeds two billion shares traded daily.

Unlike the NASDAQ, NYSE is not fully electronic. Some orders may be transmitted to the exchange by telephone. Once at the exchange, orders are filled by a specialist — a person on the trading floor whose job it is to match buyers up with sellers. This can lead to lengthy delays in filling orders, even market orders.

Because of this last point, it is recommended that the novice trader starts out trading only NASDAQ stocks. Whilst there are some spectacular moves available from NYSE stocks, the unpredictability of fills makes them less attractive. In any given trading day there are plenty of trading candidates among the NASDAQ traded stocks without needing to look at the NYSE.

Trading Hours

Both the NASDAQ and NYSE exchanges open for trading at 09:30 US Eastern Time, and close at 16:00. The NASDAQ also allows for out of hours trading with a suitable account and software, although this is an advanced topic not relevant to our strategy and therefore not something not covered in this book. Trading days are Monday to Friday, excluding public holidays.

The first half an hour of trading can be very frantic indeed, as orders that have built up overnight are executed, and any news that has occurred outside of trading hours starts to get traded into the price. Novice traders should avoid trading during this period because the market is liable to quick reversals. However, with experience, these frantic moves can give excellent profit opportunities.

The period from about 09:55 - 10:05 is often a reversal time. If prices have been rising across the board from the open, they frequently turn around and start falling in this time period. 11:00 - 11:15 is another common reversal time.

The period between 11:30 and 13:30 to 14:00 can be very quiet as US based traders go off to lunch. After 14:00 things liven up again as they come back to the market. The last hour of the session can see very high volume and good trends as everyone jumps in for the ride to the end.

In summary, the best trading times are roughly 10:00 - 12:00, and 14:00 - 16:00 Eastern Time.

Pattern Day Trader (PDT) Rules

Following the stock market tech boom of the late 1990s when many retail investors made and lost small fortunes, there were various cases of amateur traders who had lost everything, becoming violent or committing suicide because of their financial situation. In response to this, the American financial regulatory authority imposed new rules for day traders. These are the Pattern Day Trader regulations.

The rules state that any investor with a broker account balance of less than $25,000 cannot buy and sell a security on the same day more than three times in any five day rolling period. That means it is possible to buy ten different shares one day, and sell them the next, and continue to do this. But buying stock and selling it the same day is considered a day trade, and you cannot do this more than three times in any five day period, unless your account meets the minimum balance requirement.

Additionally, if you are holding a stock and the market moves against you such that if you were to liquidate your position your cash balance would be below the minimum $25,000 level, your broker must liquidate your position and you will not be allowed to trade again until you deposit the necessary funds to once again meet the required amount.

Pattern Day Trader rules apply to anyone trading American stocks regardless of the trader's nationality, country of residence, or location when making the trade. It is likely these rules will be changed in response to massive opposition and inconsistencies in the way they are applied to stocks but not futures (although given how long they have now been in place, sadly this is looking less and less likely). In the meantime, other options are available to the trader wishing to day trade without depositing $25,000 in a brokerage account. Let's have a look at those now.

Spread Bets or CFDs

Because they are derivative products, neither spread bets or CFDs are subject to the PDT rules. Both these products are readily available to European residents, but more difficult for residents of the USA to trade, due once again, to strict American regulation.

Trade Light

Another option is to make only three trades a week. Although this is not a viable long term solution, it is a way in for the novice trader. In fact, making only three day trades in any five day period is an excellent way of learning discipline and preventing over-trading, a common affliction among new traders that I mentioned in chapter twelve.

Umbrella Accounts

Umbrella accounts are not yet commonly available to UK traders, but are available in the US. Such accounts pool traders funds, and trades are then placed via the umbrella account thus circumventing the PDT rules. These accounts may also be referred to as sub-contractor accounts, or partnership accounts.

The most common way of traders funds being pooled in these types of accounts is for the trader to become a partner or shareholder in the trading firm. Their funds are placed in the company account, and all trades are paid for from that account.

Whilst this may sound complicated or difficult to manage, in reality most of it goes on in the background and from the traders perspective, they simply see a trading account as any other.

Umbrella type accounts sometimes offer additional advantages like free or discounted trading software, private chat rooms and forums for members, and may even provide greater margin that is normally permitted.

Single Stock Futures (SSFs)

These are futures contracts based on individual US stocks. They are a relatively new product, and as such suffer somewhat from a lack of liquidity and volume, and frequently have wide spreads. There are also only a limited number of SSFs available. However, as they continue to grow in popularity these will become an excellent way to trade the stock market without actually trading the stock market.

Up Tick Rule

The UpTick rule used to place certain restrictions on when it was possible to take a short position. However, from July 2007 this rule was abolished and no longer needs to be considered. It is only mentioned here for completeness. If you were previously making allowance for the uptick rule, you no longer need to do so.

Chapter 14 - The Trading Day

The trading day can be split into three parts: Pre-Market, Trading, Log and Analyse.

Our strategy requires us to find stocks that are likely to produce good (that is to say, sizeable) moves in the trading session ahead. There are around 10,000 US shares to choose from. Of these, about 5,000 - 6,000 are realistically tradable because they have sufficient volume and liquidity. We will keep a list of core trading stocks that regularly produce good moves, but the rest of the stocks we are going to watch will change on a day to day basis. The way we find them is to look for news that might affect their price, and that's done in the pre-market section of the day.

Pre-Market Homework

Our first job of the day is to find out if there are any economic announcements due. These include things like official payroll figures, new home statistics, unemployment numbers and so on.

There are lots of these reports and they can occur at various times of the day, some before the trading session, some during, and some after. It's those that occur during we are most interested in, because when figures are released they can cause wild swings in just about any market. We don't want to be in a trade when they occur, as unexpectedly good or bad numbers could cause the price of the stock we're trading to move violently, and that is an unacceptable risk.

There are lots of places to find out about economic announcements, two recommended resources are:

`http://www.bloomberg.com/markets/economic-calendar` - Bloomberg's free calendar is well laid out and easy to read. It shows you all the important times at a glance, and links to actual reports if you want to read them.

`http://www.briefing.com/investor/calendars/economic` - This is a pay site, and to trade the strategy proposed in this book you should consider a subscription. However, their economic calendar is freely available to all.

It is always worth checking two sites because it has been known for items to get left off some calendars once in a while.

Take a note of all the announcements due for the day ahead, and mark the times in a prominent position such as a sticky note on your monitor. There's no point doing the homework then forgetting about it at the crucial moment!

Tools of The Trade

Before moving on, we need to understand the concept of *tools of the trade*. Any profession — or trade — has certain tools that are required to perform it to a professional level. For example, a hairdresser will spend literally thousands of dollars on professional hair cutting scissors. Cheap scissors might look the same, but they're not up to the job of cutting hair day in day out. If the hair dresser wants to charge people money for her services, she needs to be suitably equipped. The customers will expect it, and rightly so.

Similarly, a brain surgeon will require high quality surgical instruments to perform operations. She could probably do the job with a rusty old box cutter, but would the end result be as good?

Trading is a profession like any other, and it requires its own set of tools. Some of these have already been discussed: a computer, internet connection, charting software, and a price feed. It is important to recognise that while we could use substandard cheap tools, we will — like the brain surgeon with a rusty knife — not get the same results as if we were to use professional quality tools that are designed for the job.

To put it another way, generally speaking, you get what you pay for. If we are serious about making money from trading, we need serious tools to help us do the job.

So why did I make that little speech? Well because at this point I need to introduce you to another tool of the traders profession, and it does cost money, although for the power it gives us, it is remarkably cheap.

News

The tool we need to use next is `http://briefing.com`. We saw earlier that Briefing offers us an economic calendar for free. But we need a much more powerful part of their service called In Play. This subscription service currently costs around $40 a month, with discounts available when buying a year up front. There is a thirty-day free trial available too.

There is a way to access In Play for free, although it is a crippled version. For learning purposes, it is adequate. This free version is syndicated by Yahoo Finance, and you can find it at `http://finance.yahoo.com/news/inplay-briefing-com.html` (Note: Yahoo finance has an irritating habit of changing their URLs. If the link no longer works, searching

Google or Yahoo for "Yahoo In Play Briefing" invariably provides the correct page at the top of the listings). Once you go live with your trading, I highly recommend upgrading to the full paid version of In Play directly at Briefing.com.

In Play is a constantly updated live news service that reports on anything that might affect US stock prices. News items commonly reported include company financial results, new product launches, changes to boards of directors, major new contract awards, mergers and acquisitions, and new stock placements (IPOs).

We want to look through all the news articles on the In Play page to build up a *watch list* of stocks that we think are going to produce big moves that we can trade in the upcoming session. There are a number of such news items that are of particular interest to us:

Company Financial Results

In particular, results that are better than or worse than expected by some degree. We do not assume that a company who reports better results will necessarily see their stock go up in price. It may be that analysts were expecting an even bigger increase in earnings and may therefore view the report as negative thus causing a big sell off. Our job as day traders is not to interpret the news for the likely direction of the stock, merely to find news items that are likely to make a stock move. The chart will tell us which direction it is moving in later.

Here's an example of what a company financial result news item might look like on the In Play page:

```
07:04 ABCW ABC Wireless beats by $0.05, guides Q2 revs above con-
sensus (43.59) Reports Q1 (Mar) earnings of $0.18 per share, $0.05
better than the Reuters Research consensus of $0.13; revenues rose
97.2% year/year to $41.6 mln vs the $41.1 mln consensus. Company sees
Q2 EPS of $0.15-0.16 vs consensus of $0.16 on revenues of $48-50 mln,
consensus $44 mln.
```

That might look like gibberish, but it's straightforward once you understand the shorthand and the format. Let's dissect the news item and see what it's telling us.

07:04 is the time that this item was posted on the Briefing website.

ABCW is the stock symbol for the company. This is the symbol we need to know in order to see a chart and to trade via our broker software. The price in brackets is the price of the stock at the time the news item was posted. We can see that the company in question has posted better earnings than research suggested would be the case for the last quarter. Their revenues increased almost 100% on the previous year. That sounds pretty impressive, so we're likely to see some good movement in the price in the upcoming trading session. (Note: The examples included here are all fictitious reports in the style of actual Briefing.com news items, for il-lustrative purposes.)

Raising or Lowering Guidance

This is when a company advises that it is likely to achieve earnings figures that are better than or worse than were previously expected. Again, better guidance does not necessarily mean the price will go up, and worse guidance doesn't always mean the price will drop. Here's an example:

```
08:26 MUCP Madeup-Co guides higher (22.07) Company issues upside pre
announcement for Q1 (Mar), now sees EPS of $0.09 vs Reuters consensus
of $0.06 on revenues of $60 mln, consensus $52.9 mln.
```

Here we see that Madeup-Co is now suggesting their earnings per share (EPS) will be nine cents versus a previous research consensus of six cents, so that's a 50% increase. That's prob-ably going to make this stock even more inviting to potential investors!

Upgrades and Downgrades

Analysts from institutions like Morgan Stanley, UBS and so on, publish their view on a range of stocks, such as whether they rate the stock as a "Buy", "Hold" or "Sell". Their ratings are based on much longer term anticipated price movements than we are trading, but if an an-alyst suddenly decides that a stock they had previously marked as "Hold" is now a "Strong Buy", then there is a good chance that stock is going to get a lot of interest as longer term traders pile in buying in big quantities. And of course, a lot of day traders like us will be look-ing out for just these kinds of signals as well, meaning even more likely price volatility for the stock in question. That means lots of short term price movement that we can profit from. Here is an example upgrade news item from In Play:

```
08:47 ABCC ABC Co upgraded to Strong Buy from Neutral at UBS; target
upped to $29 (22.76)
```

This is telling us that UBS (a large investment bank who employs lots of intelligent and highly paid people to analyse companies and work out their value) have published research suggest-ing to them that the stock price of ABCC should reach a target of $29. The current price is shown in brackets. UBS have upgraded the stock to a Strong Buy rating, which means they are advising their clients to buy this stock.

Many people will buy this stock just on the basis of this new rating, in the hope of selling it at the target price. Of course, we don't assume that means the price will rise; there could be plenty of people who already hold a significant amount of stock in ABC Co who will want to use this opportunity of an abundance of buyers to offload their holding and realise their profits. So we will add the stock to our watch list, but we will have no preconceptions about which direction it may go in, we will let the chart tell us all.

Pharmaceuticals

If a drug company issues a press release to say that their new cancer beating drug has performed well in trials, or has been approved by the medical authorities, that's going to mean big profits for them in the long run, and so again longer term traders are likely to start buying the stock in earnest resulting in lots of movement that we can trade.

Similarly, drug companies may report that their latest drug doesn't really work after all; we can predict the likely result! Here is an example:

```
08:47 MED MedCo - ResearchFirm says WonderDrug recommended for ap-
proval by CPMP (44.75) ResearchFirm announces that WonderDrug was
recommended for approval by the Committee for Proprietary Medicinal
Products (CPMP), the scientific advisory body of the European Agency
for the Evaluation of Medicinal Products (EMEA). This recommendation
will be forwarded to the European Commission and marks a positive
step towards European approval of WonderDrug, which is anticipated
in six months time.
```

Here the new drug "WonderDrug" has taken a step closer to being approved in Europe, so more profits are likely on the way for MedCo.

Board Level Changes

If the president of the company suddenly and unexpectedly quits for "personal reasons", or the finance officer leaves the country, the chances are they know something we don't. Such news items are rare, but we'll be wanting to watch the stock concerned when they do happen. Such an item might look like this:

```
08:08 BGR BurgerCo Chairman Jones dies of apparent heart attack
(26.93) Co announces that Chairman/CEO Fred Jones died suddenly and
unexpectedly of an apparent heart attack this morning in Orlando,
Florida, site of the BurgerCo Worldwide Owner/Operator Convention.
(Mr. Jones was 45).
```

It could be that Mr. Jones' sudden unexpected departure not only from the company but also from the world, leaves BurgerCo in a state of disarray. It could on the other hand, be interpreted as great news if he was perceived to be doing a bad job. The important thing is to understand that we don't know how investors in BurgerCo will react, but we can be pretty sure that it will cause lots of movement in the stock price, so we want to be watching.

Mergers and Acquisitions

These are a special two-for-one bonus news item. If company A announces it's interested in buying company B, then we've got two stocks to keep an eye on. For example:

```
08:19 AAAC AardvardCo to acquire BobbyCo (BBBC) for $49 mln (40.79)
BobbyCo Inc is a privately-held, New York based company that is the
leading provider of software solutions for Bluetooth wireless prod-
ucts.
```

Again, this could be seen in both a positive and negative light for each of the companies involved in the deal. We'll be watching so we can take advantage either way.

Building The List

As you'll discover, there can be lots of news items every day, particularly around earnings season when companies report their quarterly financials. Clearly we'll need to filter the news somehow, so that we end up with a manageable list of stocks to watch. When selecting stocks to potentially trade, we are looking for those that historically:

- Are priced in the region $20 - $100 (although we'll consider lower priced ones if the news is big).
- Have good daily volume, ideally at least 1 - 1.5 million shares
- Have good daily travel range, $1 or more.

How do we check these three things? Well the price is easy, Briefing gives us that in the news story, so that's our first filter dealt with. For each remaining news item we're interested in, we'll put its symbol into our charting software and have a look back over the last few days' charts. All charting packages should show volume. If a stocks recent volume is lower than the 1 to 1.5 million shares traded daily that we want, we may still want to consider watching it if the news is strong enough to suggest there will be considerable activity in it in the coming trading session.

The final criteria is travel range. This means the distance that the stock price moves from its lowest point to its highest point during any given day. If we look back at the chart that we first saw in Part One (see opposite), we can see that the travel range for the day was about 80 cents, i.e. the distance from the highest point, 1, to the lowest point, 2.

Once again, if the news is particularly important then we may still want to watch the stock even if the travel range is historically too small.

Those news stocks meeting all of the above criteria will then go onto our daily watch list. We're looking for around ten to fifteen stocks, twenty at most. Too many means we'll spend too much time looking at them all and are likely to miss any moves. Too few means we might not find anything worth trading.

When you first start out you may well find that you have difficulty in keeping your watch list down to under twenty stocks. With so many to choose from, it can be tempting to want to watch them all. If that happens, then here's a remedy.

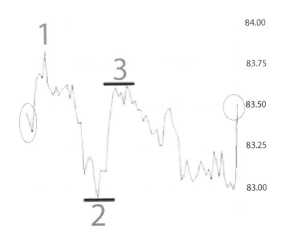

With each stock you note on your list, give it a score from 1 to 5, where 1 means you think the news item for this stock is not that important, and 5 means it's really important. When you've completed the list, take the top twenty stocks with the highest scores, and use those as your watch list.

When the market is closed for the day, go back through all of the stocks you noted (including those you later discarded). For each one, bring up a chart for the day, and find the original news item. Compare your score and the news item with the chart and see how the news actually affected that stock.

Do this for all the stocks, every day for at least two weeks. Each day you'll be fine-tuning your news-radar and learning exactly what effect different types of news have on different types of stocks. Yes it's a bit of work, but it's a skill that you will have for life, and a highly profitable one at that.

The free version of Briefing's In Play syndicated by Yahoo Finance, is artificially delayed. We can certainly use it to learn to read the news feed, and we can even use it to build our watch list of stocks. When we go live with our trading though, we'll be behind the curve, missing out on the most recent (and therefore most relevant) stories. This is why I recommend upgrading to the paid service when ready to trade live.

Gappers

News stocks should be our priority as they have the most reason to put in strong moves. However, we can add to these any stocks that are gapping up or down. These are stocks that open at a price some distance from where they closed at the end of the previous trading day.

Roughly around 70% of gaps are filled, which is to say that during the trading session the price will come back to meet the closing price of the previous session. If a gap open price is within the previous day's trading range then it has an 85% chance of being filled.f

There is a good chance that some of the news stocks already picked from Briefing.com will gap at the open, but Briefing very kindly provides us with a list of gappers in its In Play section about twenty minutes before the market opens (these are stocks that have already moved in pre-market trading). These should be checked as well.

Market Sentiment

As we go through our pre-market homework, we need to be building an overall picture of the market sentiment for the day, that is to say, whether the feeling is generally bullish or bearish. Briefing helps here as well by giving a summary of what has happened in the morning on the European and Asian markets. If these have moved strongly in one direction, they will affect sentiment in the United States. It also reports on what has been happening to the futures during the overnight period. Because futures trade 24 hours, they can provide a constant indicator of sentiment (we'll look at another use for futures later).

So for example, if Europe and Asia both fell heavily overnight, the futures are down, and Microsoft came out with an earnings warning, it's pretty likely that the market will drop at the open. This does not necessarily mean it will go down for the rest of the session, but it gives us an idea that the overall bias is probably negative, and as such we'll be more prepared to find opportunities trading to the short side.

Further Sources

There are other ways of finding stocks that are moving well once the market is open. These can be particularly useful when trading the later part of the session.

FinViz HeatMap (`http://finviz.com/map.ashx`) displays stock prices visually, graded by percentage change up or down. The figures are delayed, but are useful for finding what has been moving during the day (a paid upgrade gets real time prices should you want them). You can zoom in and look at individual sectors, or zoom out and see the whole market in one go. A useful tool for people who like to see data visually.

FinViz Screener (`http://finviz.com/screener.ashx`) has a vast array of ways of filtering stocks by volume and price. Again, the prices are delayed, but the service is handy for finding stocks that have moved strongly. Of particular interest is the Unusual Volume signal which shows stocks being traded in larger quantities than normal. The FinViz screener can even try and find basic patterns like double tops and bottoms, head and shoulders, and triangles. It's not a substitute for doing our own homework, but it certainly has a place in the trader's toolkit.

Yahoo Stock Center (`http://finance.yahoo.com/stock-center`) gives a nice overview of what's moving, including most active stocks, and biggest percentage gainers and losers. The Trending Tickers section has in interesting additional social element in that it shows stocks that are attracting unusual levels of interest from other users of Yahoo Finance.

eSignal's scanner (`http://www.esignal.com`), unlike the previous options which are free, is quite an expensive service. It allows you to quickly scan every US share based on criteria such as price trading above or below its first hour or last hour range.

These sources are of most use for finding trades in the later part of the day. Stocks that moved strongly in the morning often retrace some of that move towards the end of the day, and scanners can tell you about those earlier moves. But for trading the morning, it is always better to use Briefing's In Play to find news driven stocks before they make their move. Scanners can only ever tell you what already happened. If a stock shows up on a scanner, it's because it made a move, and that was probably the move we wanted to be trading. The pre-market news tells you what's likely to happen before it does, which means we can watching and waiting ready to pounce — and profit.

Core Trading Stocks

I mentioned earlier that in addition to the daily watch list of news stocks, we will keep a list of core trading stocks. Ideally we want about five or six stocks that we know tend to move well each day — that is that they cover a good range, have good volume, and usually move in a trending rather than sideways pattern.

By having these same stocks on our watch list at all times, we will always have something to keep an eye on even on slower news days when we can't find quite so many new opportunities (although there are always some). Our primary stocks to watch each day will always be our newly selected news stocks, the core stocks just provide a little backup.

When you first start trading, you won't have any core trading stocks, you will need to build up a list over time. To do this, each time you find a new news stock, take a look back at some charts for that stock covering the last few weeks. You can quickly see from looking at them if the stock regularly makes patterns that you can trade.

Over the course of a few weeks you'll start to notice a few stocks that crop up time and again as you go through the In Play news. Even more so if you use the scoring system described earlier, to fine tune your news reading abilities. These will become your core trading stocks.

Review your core stock list regularly. If you have a stock on the list that no longer produces good trades, consider replacing it with something that is working better. Try and keep the core list to a maximum of five or six stocks, it's important that it doesn't distract too much from the main task of watching news stocks.

Trading

We'll now look at some very specific chart patterns that work consistently on the US market, and are used every day by professional US Stock traders. I've used them for more than ten years, and they work as well today as the day I learnt them. Because they are based on price action and not some short-lived fashionable indicator or other, they work reliably, consistently, and will continue to do so as long as human beings are participating in the market.

We are going to look at two sets of patterns, those that are suited to the early part of the day, and those which work well in the later part. There is no doubt that there are bigger profits to be had in the mornings, simply because that's when most volume is traded. However, not everyone has access to the market at those hours, and there is still plenty of opportunity later on. For European based traders in particular, the time difference means it's entirely possible to work a day job and then be back at home in time to trade the last hour of the US market. Here are the patterns we are going to study:

Early session patterns:
- ERBO - Early Range BreakOut
- OR - Opening Reversal

- 1234 Consolidation

Late session patterns:

- 1234 Consolidation
- Previous Days Range BreakOut
- Triangles

As we look at these patterns, it is important to keep in mind the basic principals of trend, support, and resistance that were covered in Part One of this book. If a pattern says "Buy!", but the chart shows that there is obvious resistance a short way from the price, clearly this will affect the risk : reward ratio and it is probably not a good trade. We'll also look later at some other less traditional indicators that should be used to confirm these patterns.

The examples I will show are all based on 5 minute charts. Other timeframes can be used, but 5 minutes works well with the patterns described here. They're what I use, and what I recommend. Sticking with a single timeframe helps you fix the patterns in your mind. They can look quite different if you suddenly switch to a 1 minute or 10 minute chart.

Exiting Trades

The patterns I will introduce to you will show you when to enter a trade. But we also need to know when to exit. Indeed, exiting a trade at the right time can make huge differences in profit or loss. Remember, we need to run winning trades as long as possible to extract as much profit as we can. Good exits will help, so let's look at how we will decide where to close our trades.

In addition to watching the price for support and resistance areas which can signal trade exits, we are also going to use a 10 period Exponential Moving Average (calculated on the close price) on our charts. You will see that once a move has started, the 10 EMA will often contain the price until that move is over, which is to say the price will remain solidly on one side of that EMA. Therefore any subsequent break of the EMA can provide an excellent exit signal. Another way we can use this EMA is to exit the trade once it goes flat for a few bars, which suggests the end of a trend.

The EMA isn't just useful in exits, it can also come in handy when a trade is setting up. In some examples you will notice that the price is already contained within the EMA before the trade is signalled, making it even more likely to be successful.

Whole number dollar amounts (e.g. $35.00, then $36.00 and so on) are very important when trading US stocks. Decade numbers ($10, $20, $30 etc) even more so. If the price hits a whole number and stalls, it is often a good place to exit all or part of a trade. When assessing the risk : reward ratio of a potential trade, the proximity of whole numbers should be taken into account. We should effectively consider whole numbers as pre-defined support and resistance lines, and decade numbers as even stronger support and resistance.

In the absence of any obvious technical level at which to exit, we can use a *3-bar* exit. It's a simple strategy, stay in the trade until you see three consecutive bars or candles go against you (so three down bars if you are long, three up bars if you are short), then exit. Three consecutive bars against you usually indicates a change in trend, or at least a period of consolidation.

Never ever let a profit turn into a loss. If a trade starts to turn against you, it is better to exit with a small profit than wait to see it evaporate and then turn into a losing position. If it turns around again, you can always get back into the trade. If once you have entered the trade, it doesn't follow through very quickly, or turns against you, jump out immediately. There is no shame in taking a loss; the market is always right. The important thing is to get out with as small a loss as possible so you are there ready for the next trade. There is nothing worse than watching a small loss grow into a bigger one.

Comfort Exit

It is often a good idea to exit half a position instead of ending the trade completely, a process known as *scaling out*. For example, if you are long 500 shares and come up against resistance at a whole number, consider selling 250 shares instead of closing the entire position. Leave the rest of the position open to run on to the next logical price target.

Scaling out eases the psychological pressure on you the trader because once half out you have some profit locked in. I call this a *comfort-exit* because it makes it much more comfortable to stay in a trade when we know we've already banked some profit. You can then leave the other half extra wiggle room because you have already taken some money off the table.

Stop Loss

Always place a stop order as soon as you have entered a trade. It will help psychologically because it will take you out of the trade automatically if it goes against you, and it will protect you if you suddenly have a technical problem that means you cannot exit the trade yourself. A stop order used in this way is called a *stop loss*, because it literally stops your loss exceeding a certain amount.

10 cents is a good initial stop loss if there are no obvious technical areas to place one. You should not wait for your stop order to be hit if the trade doesn't go your way, always try and exit manually first. Consider the stop order as your emergency exit in case things go drastically wrong. It should be the most you are prepared to lose, but it's always much better

to acknowledge the trade is not good and get out manually with a smaller loss if possible. Smaller losses are easier to recover from. Taking a loss manually will also make you stronger as a trader.

Trade Pattern — ERBO — Early Range BreakOut

As has already been mentioned, the early part of the trading session can see frantic trading activity. The highs and lows set by the price during this period can become defining ranges for the rest of the day. If the price subsequently breaks out of its early range, it will often do so with great force, and momentum will push it on further. As more traders see the price shoot off, greed will cause them to jump on the bandwagon, pushing the price onwards even more.

There are three early ranges we are interested in: the first 20 minutes of the session, the first half an hour, and the first hour. Of these, the first half an hour is the most preferable to trade as it avoids being in a trade during the common reversal times of 10:00 and 11:00.

For a half hour range, we draw on the chart a horizontal line at the highest price the stock has traded at in the first 30 minutes of the trading session, and another line at the lowest price in that period. For the 20 minute and one hour ranges, we use the highest and lowest prices set in the first 20 minutes and first 60 minutes of the trading session to determine where to draw our horizontal lines.

In all three cases we are assuming that these high and low prices have become support and resistance. The lines we have drawn on the chart show this support and resistance clearly to us. If the price breaks above the resistance line after the first 30 minutes, we go long. If it breaks below the support line, we go short. In both cases, we will seek confirmation of the trade from the time and sales screen before entering, something we will look at in detail a little later. For now, let's look more at this pattern.

Once again, 10:00 is a reversal time, so if you trade a 20 minute range breakout at 09:55 there is a strong chance the trade will turn against you 5 minutes later. For this reason it is *highly advisable* to stick to using the 30 minute range for at least your first six months trading, until you have some solid experience under your belt.

The best range breakouts occur when there is a clear bias towards the high or low of the range before the break occurs, as we will see in the examples.

Risk : Reward

When trading these patterns, because we are expecting the price to follow through very quickly, we will know very soon if the pattern has failed. In other words, if the price breaks out of the early range but does not subsequently continue in the same direction, but instead moves back inside the range, we know the pattern has failed. Thus the risk we accept can be very small indeed. We should be able to exit the trade with a loss of between 5 - 10 cents. The exact figure will depend on the stock being traded and the spread on that stock, and how far from the breakout level we actually enter the trade.

Reward is slightly more difficult to calculate. Unlike the patterns we looked at in Part One, these range breakout patterns do not predict a price target. However, we can look at pre-existing support and resistance lines on the chart (including whole and decade numbers), and use those to assess how far the price may run. Thus if we are accepting a risk of 10 cents on the trade, we want to be sure that there are no support or resistance lines within 20 cents of the entry point in order to meet our risk:reward criteria.

ERBO Examples

An opening range defined by the high and low prices set in the first n minutes of trading, and the price showing bias towards the high, then breaking out:

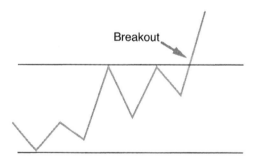

Here the price is biased towards the low:

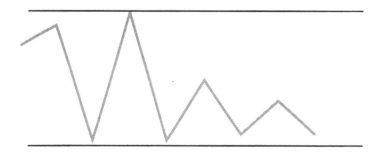

In the two previous examples the price showed clear bias towards one side of the opening range. Any subsequent break in the direction of that bias has a good chance of success. In this next example there is no bias after the range is set. A breakout may still occur, but has less chance of following through because the stock has not shown any tendency to go either up or down:

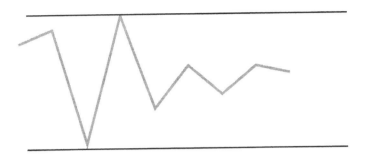

ERBO Example 1

In this first example we see a first half hour early range breakout on a 5 minute chart. The dotted vertical line marks the start of the session. We can see that the assumed resistance and support lines have been drawn in at the high and low points set in the 30 minutes of trading:

The price is showing a clear bias towards the lower line, suggesting a break of the support line and a possible short trade. Notice that the EMA contains most of the price as it falls towards the bottom of the range, adding to the probability of follow through on a breakout. The support line is at about $89.80, so the next whole number is $89.00, which is 80 cents away. If we were to accept 10 cents as the risk on this trade, and use the whole number as our target price, then we have a potential risk:reward ratio of 1:8.

To trade this pattern we would have put in sell order once the price broke below the support line. For entering a new trade we would prefer to use a limit order, perhaps specifying a price of $89.75. If the price drops very quickly following the breakout, our limit order limits the slippage we could suffer. The tradeoff of course, is that we might not get filled. Even so, missing out on the trade by not getting filled is preferable to entering at a price far from where we wanted to enter due to massive slippage.

We would wait until the price broke through the support by a couple of cents or more. A single trade that occurred a cent or two below the line would not be sufficient evidence of a break. So we would watch the time and sales (which shows us the last price in real time, more on this in a moment) and when we saw a string of trades occur at prices below the line, we would place our order. Let's assume we got our entry order filled at $89.75. We'd now need to decide where to exit. In fact there are several possible exits on this chart:

- The whole number of $89. This would give us a profit of 70 cents per share.
- Three bars against us, which would be an exit at about $89.40 for a profit of 35 cents per share.
- A break of the EMA at $89.50, for a profit of 25 cents a share.
- Any combination of the above if we decided to scale out.

If we were trading 1000 shares, then the smallest profit this trade would have made would be $250 (1000 x 25 cents) and the biggest would be $700 (1000 x 70 cents.) Not bad for about 15 minutes in the market.

ERBO Example 2

This chart shows another early range breakout, this time with price showing a bias to the high before it breaks through the resistance line, shown by the ellipse. Again, the 10 EMA contains the price up to the breakout, adding to the probability of follow through.

The nearest whole number above the resistance line is 50 cents away, so we can hope for at least 50 cents profit. Even if we wanted to give the trade plenty of room to work out, a maximum 20 cent risk would still give us a risk:reward ratio of 1:2.5. However, a better way to limit the risk on this trade would be to place a stop order just below the EMA which was about 10 cents away at the time of the breakout.

Let's assume we entered at $45.50. Once again, there were a number of possible exits for this trade:

- We could have exited all or half of our position at $46.00, the whole number resistance line, but we can see that the price blasted straight through that. On 1000 shares traded, we would have made $500 (1000 x 50 cents) if we chose to exit all the position here.

- We could have hung on, and then used the 3-bar rule and exited all or half the trade when three bars went against us. If we exited all the position at the bottom of the third candle (point 1 on the chart), which was about $46.40, we would have made $900 profit on 1000 shares (1000 x 90 cents).

- There was another whole number at $47 (point 2), so again we could have used that to exit for a profit of $1500 on 1000 shares.

- Finally, if we chose to run at least some of the trade until the EMA was broken, we'd still be in the trade at the very end of this chart (point 3)! On 1000 shares, we'd be $1800 better off, and still in the trade.

Ideally we would have used a combination of the above, exiting half the trade as a comfort exit, and running the other half until the EMA was broken.

Trade Pattern — OR — Opening Reversal

This pattern is a variation on the Early Range BreakOut, and one that specifically applies to gappers. Remember a gapper is a share whose price has opened up or down from the previous day's close, creating a gap in the chart.

If the price gaps up and then breaks out of its early range to the downside, many traders will short the stock in the hope that it will close the gap. This adds to the downward pressure. The same applies in reverse to stocks that gap down and then break out to the upside.

If the stock gaps up (presumably on good news) and then breaks out to the upside of the early range, traders who have until that point avoided buying for fear of the gap being filled, will see that this is now unlikely and will jump on board, adding to the upwards momentum. Again, the same applies in reverse to gaps down.

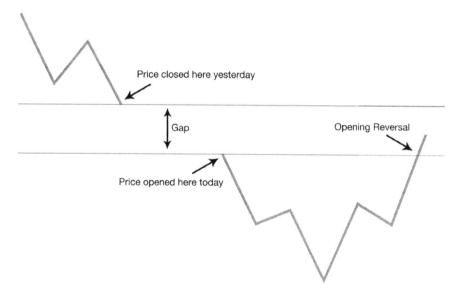

Here the price gaps down (opens below yesterday's close) and keeps going down, then reverses and breaks up past the open. This is the sign to buy. Yesterday's close would make a good initial target for this trade.

In the next diagram the price gaps down (opens below the previous day's close) but this time it starts to rise. However, it fails to close the gap, and once it reverses and takes out its low, it is time to take the short.

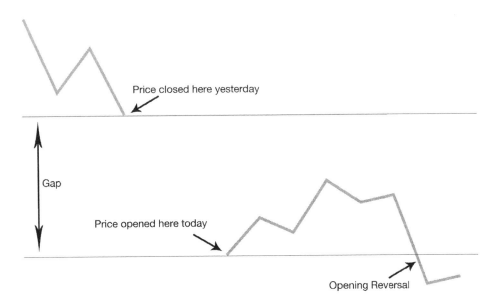

The next diagram shows the same story but in reverse for a gap up. When traders see the gap fail to close, more will start buying, helping the price break above the opening high.

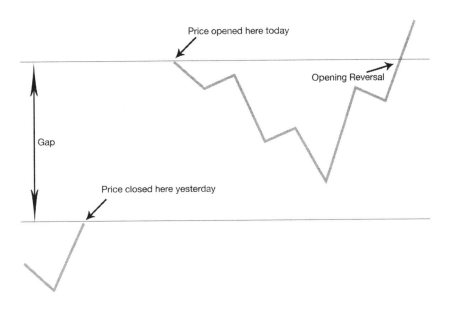

Now for some real chart examples. The vertical line on this first chart marks the end of the previous trading session and the start of today's session.

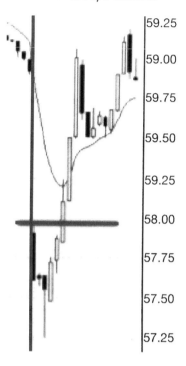

At the open the price gaps down but soon breaks out to the upside of the early range. As with the Early Range BreakOuts, I have drawn in the assumed resistance line at the highest price set during the first 20 minutes of trading.

We would have had to have been careful going long (buying) here because there was a whole number ($58) just above the resistance line. We could have left our entry a little late to ensure the price cleared the whole number, so we'll assume we bought at $58.10.

Our logical target is the closing price of the previous day, which we can see is approximately $58.90, so we know we have good risk:reward ratio because our target price is 80 cents away from our entry. As we can see on the chart, the stock easily made the target price, so we could have sold all our shares at $58.90 giving us a profit of 80 cents per share, which is $400 when trading 500 shares, $800 trading 1000 shares, $1600 trading 2000 shares, and so on.

In the next example (see opposite) the price gaps up, i.e. it opens at the start of the session higher than it closed at the end of the previous session.

It tries to go lower and close the gap (i.e. meet up with the closing price of yesterday's session) but fails, and instead breaks the early range to the upside.

There were three good options for exiting this trade:

- The break of the EMA
- The whole numbers at $93 and $94 (ideal for a comfort exit)
- The 3-bar rule which would have got us out around $93.60.

Even exiting at the first whole number of $93 would have yielded a profit of at least 50 cents a share, which is $250 when trading 500 shares.

Trade Pattern — 1234 Consolidation

This pattern works in both early and late parts of the trading session. It comprises four 5 minute bars at (or very close to) the day's high or low.

For 1234 consolidation at the high of the day, we are looking for it to occur just above a whole number which will provide support; this signals a potential long trade. For the pattern to be valid at the low of the day, signalling a potential short trade, it should occur just below a whole number (providing resistance).

The entry is taken after the fourth bar completes, going long once the price exceeds the high set by the fourth bar of the pattern (when the pattern occurs at the high of the day), or short when it exceeds the low of the fourth bar (when the pattern occurs at the low of the day).

In this pattern, the bulls (in an up-trend) are taking a breather, but the bears do not have sufficient strength to bring the price back down. In other words, although there are not enough buyers to push the price any higher, the sellers are even lower in number and cannot push it below the whole number. Hence it's only a matter of time before the price goes up again. The same is true in reverse for shorts.

Let's see an example. In the box we can see consolidation after a price rise, just above a whole number. We would look to buy on the fifth bar as the price exceeds the high of the fourth bar.

The logical place to exit this trade was at the decade number of $60 which we know will be strong resistance, so our profit if we bought at $59.20 would be 80 cents per share (which is $400 when trading 500 shares).

The ERBO and OR patterns, by their nature, are for use in the early part of the trading day. The 1234 consolidation pattern can be used in the morning or afternoon to equal effect. Now let's examine a couple of patterns that work well in the later part of the day.

Trade Pattern — Previous Day's Range

The highest price, lowest price, and to some extent the closing price of the previous day's trading session are very important levels of support and resistance in the US market. Most decent chart software can automatically display lines at these levels. If an ERBO or OR pattern breaks through the previous day's high or low then they are likely to have momentum and go even further.

Breaks of the previous day's range on their own can also give good trading opportunities in the later part of the day, after lunch.

Additionally, the previous day's high, low, and close can provide a good exit point for half or all of a position when trading any of the patterns. Let's look at some examples.

In this chart the lower line (at $31.13) indicates the previous day's closing price, and the upper line (at $31.34) the previous day's high. Note that once the price gets into the zone between these lines it bounces around within it for some time. Indeed, before the breakout occurs, the current day's high is the same as yesterday's high, so we know if the price breaks above $31.34 it has a good chance of going higher. This is exactly what happens.

Had we bought on this breakout, then in the absence of any obvious technical reason to exit, we could have sold just before the market closed at the end of the chart for a gain of at least 30 cents per share giving a profit of $150 when trading 500 shares, or $300 when trading 1000.

In this next example the upper line ($24.68) is the previous day's close, and the lower line ($24.30) the previous day's low:

After the early drop, the price slowly makes its way back up but cannot get through the previous day's close (resistance). It falls back, consolidates just above the previous day's low, and then falls through it and drops about 70 cents giving plenty of opportunity for profit.

Exercise Questions

1. Can you see an early range breakout pattern on this chart?

2. What was the entry?

3. What would have been a good exit?

4. Where could you have placed an initial stop?

5. Can you see a reversal pattern?

6. Where was the confirmation?

Answers

1. The early range breakout is marked by the box number 1. Notice how the low of the early range coincides with the previous day's low. This confluence of support lines makes the support stronger, and any eventual breakout even more important.

2. The entry was around $24.28 when the price broke through the low set in the first 30 minutes of trading.

3. There were two possible whole number exits shown by the boxes numbered 2.

4. The initial stop could have been 10 cents for this pattern. If the price retraced by that amount we would know the breakout had not followed through.

5. There is a double bottom reversal shown here by the arrows numbered 3.

6. Confirmation of the double bottom occurred when the price exceeded the previous high, marked here by the bottom horizontal line, number 4.

Here's another example chart:

In this chart the top line at $62.92 is the previous day's high, and the bottom line at $61.39 is the previous day's close.

Exercise Questions

1. What early entry pattern can you see?

2. What was the entry?

3. What was a good exit point?

4. Where would your initial stop have been?

Answers

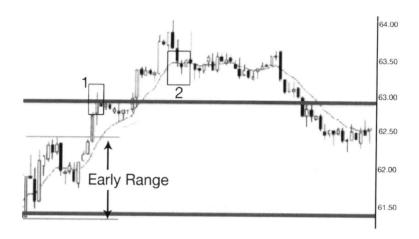

1. By drawing in the high and low of the early range, it becomes easy to see that the early entry pattern was an Early Range BreakOut.

2. The entry was on a break of the early range high, which was around $62.50.

3. There are two clear resistance points very close to each other, which make an ideal exit:
   - The previous day's high at $62.92
   - The whole number of $63 (marked by the box number 1).

When multiple support or resistance lines converge like this they become even stronger because collectively more people will be paying attention to them. We can see that the price did indeed have difficulty getting through this area, although ultimately the stock was strong enough to break through and continue higher. It would have been perfectly valid to sell half the position at around $63 and hang on to the other half until the price broke down through the 10 EMA at the area shown in the box number 2, which would have given an additional 50 cents per share on the remaining position.

4. The initial stop would be just behind the entry. 10 cents would be sufficient to know whether or not the breakout was following through.

Triangles

Triangle patterns, as described in Part One of this book, work well in both early and late parts of the trading session, but are best applied to the late session because we have other set ups to concentrate on in the morning.

Here's an example:

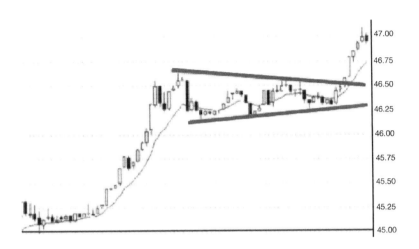

This triangle took a long time to set up, partly because it was forming during the slower lunchtime part of the day. The breakout when it happened though, was rapid. An exit around the whole number of $47 would have given a profit of about $500 on 1000 shares. Notice that the triangle itself also gave a profit target of about the same amount.

Additional Indicators

There are some further less traditional indicators we can and should look at before entering a trade:

- Support and resistance levels
- Time and sales
- Relevant futures
- Market internals and the advance decline line
- Sectors

We've already covered support and resistance, so let's take a look at each of the others in more detail.

Time And Sales

Time and sales is a critical indicator when trading the Early Range BreakOut and Opening Reversal patterns. Both of these patterns rely on *momentum* to keep pushing the price onwards once a breakout has occurred. Whilst the patterns themselves will alert you to a possible trade, it is the time and sales screen which will determine whether or not to actually enter that trade. Its importance in trading those two patterns cannot be overstated.

So what is time and sales? If we think back to Part One of this book, we looked at how every trade that takes place is reported via the last price. A time and sales screen is a list of these last prices as they occur in real time. In other words it shows every trade that has taken place for a particular stock.

The screen shows us the time the trade was made, the price, and the size of the trade (the number of shares traded). If we see a lot of big trades going through quickly at the ask, then the ask price is probably going to go up in the not-too-distant future as the sellers at that price run out of stock or shift their price. And of course, the reverse is true if we see lots of big trades go through at the bid.

As we watch the time and sales (which is also referred to as the *tape*, because before the time of computers trades were reported in real time on a punched paper tape), we can build up an idea of momentum. If the price is rising, and we are still seeing lots of trades going through at the ask, or the speed of those trades is accelerating, then clearly the momentum is upwards.

Time and sales gives us confirmation for breakout trades. If the breakout occurs on good momentum, it is much more likely to follow through. If, on the other hand, the price breaks out but we can see lots of trades occurring in the opposite direction, we will want to steer clear of the trade.

Most charting packages provide time and sales information, and most also allow you to colour code it to make it much easier to get a quick idea of which way momentum is building. You should configure your time and sales screen to show only trades, not orders, because not all orders are filled. You want it to show all trades that occur at or above the ask price in green, and those at or below the bid in red.

Opposite is an example of what a time and sales screen will look like when configured in the manner suggested. In the example we can see roughly the last twenty trades that have occurred for this stock, the prices they went through at, and the number of shares traded in each transaction. Note that the size is reported in lots of 10, so a size of 100 means 1000 shares were traded (100 lots of 10).

Time	Price	Size
10:02:06	25.42	100
10:02:06	25.42	100
10:02:06	25.42	600
10:02:06	25.42	200
10:02:05	**25.41**	**300**
10:02:05	**25.41**	**300**
10:02:05	**25.41**	**300**
10:02:05	**25.41**	**200**
10:02:05	25.42	500
10:02:05	25.42	600
10:02:05	25.42	200
10:02:05	25.42	300
10:02:05	25.42	500
10:02:05	25.42	200
10:02:05	25.42	1000
10:02:05	25.42	400
10:02:05	25.42	300
10:02:05	25.42	200
10:02:05	25.42	1000
10:02:05	25.42	500
10:02:05	25.42	200
10:02:05	25.42	500
10:02:05	25.42	1000

The screen has been colour coded in the way suggested above, so trades at or above the ask price are in green and trades at the bid price or below are in red. Very quickly it is possible to see that there are lots more trades at the ask price, and at bigger sizes, than at the bid price. This suggests momentum at this instant in time is upwards.

If we were looking at a chart that we thought was about to break out to the downside (a potential short trade) and saw a time and sales screen like the one in this example, we would not want to go short because clearly there is much more buying than selling going on. On the other hand, if our potential trade were a long, then this screen would act as good confirmation for that trade.

It is important to understand that time and sales should not just be used as a snapshot, looking at it once before entering a trade. By watching trades going through and the speed at which they do so, we can tell a lot about momentum. If the tape is moving slowly, not many trades are occurring, there is no momentum, so a breakout has less chance of following through. If the tape speeds up as it approaches the breakout price, it suggests more and more traders are getting involved in the stock, which will help it to break through the resistance or support.

Once we're well into the trade, and we've seen that the momentum has carried the price on and we are in profit, we no longer need to watch the time and sales. Its usefulness to us is over and we can turn our attention back to the chart where we can watch out for the exit signals we have already discussed.

It takes time to learn to read the tape, but as I have already mentioned, it is essential to trading the Early Range BreakOut and Opening Reversal patterns. The chart *suggests* the trade, the time and sales provides the confirmation to enter it, the final *go / no-go* decision.

It is something that must be learnt by experience, much like driving a car. When you first learn to drive you have to learn stopping distances. You read these long tables that tell you about how far ahead you have to brake at a certain speeds and in certain road conditions. The theory's all there, but you have to actually do it to learn that instinctive feel for when to brake. I imagine that nobody who has passed their driving test thinks about stopping distances consciously each time they brake, they've learnt the way the car behaves, and it has become a natural instinct to know when to start to brake, how hard to press the brake pedal, and so forth. Time and sales is a lot like that. I can only teach you so much in this book. From there, you have to paper trade (more on that later), and keep at it until you get it. It will take a while, but the more you do it, the easier it becomes. Soon you'll be able to watch the tape and you won't be consciously thinking *"Where's the momentum? More buys or sells? Bigger buys or bigger sells?"*, you'll just have that same instinctive feel for it as you have when driving a car. And as with learning to read the In Play news, it is another very profitable skill that once acquired, you will have for life.

Relevant Futures

First, a quick refresher on futures. A futures contract is a contract between a buyer and seller, for a seller to deliver to the buyer a certain quantity of the underlying asset at a future date, at a price agreed now.

The key point here is that the futures contract is for a price agreed *now*, not some price that someone thinks might exist in the future. That is to say, the word *future* refers to when the underlying goods on which the contract has been taken out, will be delivered.

Why are we interested in futures if we are trading stocks? Because they can give us some very big hints about what is going to happen to stock prices.

There exist in the financial markets, so-called indices, which summarise market direction. Examples of such indices are the FTSE 100, S&P 500, and the Dow Jones Industrial Average. These indices comprise a number of blue chip stocks that can be thought of as being a broadly representative sample of the market as a whole. TV news shows and newspapers love to quote these indices at us every day, they give us a quick idea of whether stock prices are generally rising or falling. If more stocks in the market are going up than down, the value of that market's index should rise.

There also exist futures contracts based on these indices. So for example it is possible to buy and sell futures contracts based on the value of the FTSE 100 index, the S&P 500, or the CAC40. We can view the prices of these contracts in exactly the same way we watch stock prices in order to get an idea of overall market sentiment.

Here's the interesting thing. The futures contracts for a given index are more efficient than the index itself. If market sentiment turns negative, it takes time for traders to sell off the stocks that make up the index, and therefore for that index to fall in value. Futures traders on the other hand, will already have sold off their contracts, and so the futures price will have fallen quickly. So in fact, futures prices can be thought of as a *leading indicator* of market sentiment. They can give us a brief glimpse of what is to come.

How do we use the futures? There are two contracts we are interested in, the E-Mini S&P 500 (often referred to simply by its ticker symbol of "ES"), which is indicative of sentiment on the NYSE exchange, and the E-Mini NASDAQ 100 (known as the "NQ"), which will reflect sentiment on the NASDAQ.

As we've already seen, many factors affect stock prices, not just news but also market sentiment. If the market as a whole is rising rapidly, stocks that are already going up will tend to go up more quickly as buyers get carried away in the positive sentiment, and stocks that have no overall direction may also rise a little. Stocks that are going down will do so more slowly. Think of market sentiment as a magnet that exerts a pull on all stocks.

Quite simply then, when we are going long we want to see the futures contract relevant to our stock going up. And naturally, we want to see it going down if we are going short. With purely news driven stocks, the futures direction is less important, but with enough stocks to choose from, why take the chance of going against the market sentiment? We at least want the futures to be going sideways rather than against us.

There is another benefit to watching futures. If our stock is poised to break out and the futures suddenly shoot upwards, there is a very high probability our stock will follow a few seconds later. So if we see such a move we need to be ready to pull the trigger and enter our trade. Similarly, if the futures drop suddenly whilst we are already in a long trade, we will need to be very careful and get ready to jump out at the slightest sign of a slowdown.

Sudden big movements in futures prices then, can give us a few seconds advance warning of movements in the price of the stock that we are watching. Those few seconds can be enough to get us in or out of a trade before the rest of the market realises what's happening. While everyone else jumps on board, we're already in the trade and can sit back and enjoy the ride!

Market Internals

Depending on the charting software we are using, we will have access to various numerical values that tell us what is going on in the market as a whole. These numbers are much less important than the time and sales and the futures, but they can be useful to keep an eye on if we want extra confirmation of the best direction to trade in.

The numbers we are interested in are:

- Up Volume / Down Volume
- Advancing Issues / Declining Issues:
- Sectors

We'll take a look at each in turn.

Up Volume / Down Volume

These figures tell us quite literally how many shares have been traded in stocks that are rising in price and how many in stocks that are falling in price.

As the day progresses the numbers will obviously become very large. There are two sets of these numbers, one for combined up and down volume of all NYSE stocks and one for all NASDAQ stocks. If the stock we are interested in trading is on the NASDAQ, we'll want to be looking at the NASDAQ up / down volume. If the up volume is twice as much as the down volume, we may assume that market sentiment at that point in time, is more bullish than bearish and so we would be favouring long-side trades. However, these numbers are changing all the time and if you decide to use them it is important to keep an eye on how they are moving in relation to each other rather than take a snapshot look at them.

Here's a quick example. If the up volume is 45 million and the down volume 20 million, we might assume bullish conditions. However if 10 minutes later the numbers are now up volume 50 million and down volume 40 million, it becomes clear that there has been a huge amount of selling over that last ten minute period. Use with caution.

Advancing Issues / Declining Issues

These numbers tell us how many stocks are currently trading at higher prices than their opening price (advancing issues) and how many are lower than their opening price (declining issues).

Again there are two sets of numbers available to us, one to cover NYSE stocks and one for NASDAQ. And again it is important to watch for changes in these numbers rather than take a snapshot. To help us do that, we can plot a chart of the *advance / decline* line. This line indicates the number of advancing issues minus the declining issues. A positive figure indicates a rising market and a negative figure a falling one.

There are, of course, advance / decline lines for each exchange, and we are interested in those for the NYSE and the NASDAQ. The symbols for plotting these lines on a chart tend to be specific to particular charting packages.

Example:

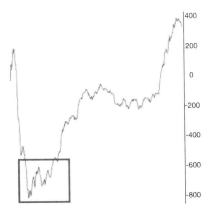

This chart shows the advance / decline line over a complete trading day. We see that the market opened slightly up, but then fell away very sharply. We can apply standard basic technical analysis to this chart to get an idea of where it might be headed, and note that after making a double bottom reversal pattern in the area highlighted, the line started going back up indicating buying was going on across the market as a whole.

By keeping an eye on this chart it becomes clear that if we wanted to trade in the same direction as the market as a whole, then short positions were preferable for the first hour or so, and then long positions for much of the rest of the day.

Sectors

Just as there are indices that reflect sentiment across the exchange as a whole, there are also sub-indices which comprise stocks in particular market sectors such as software, transport, or energy.

If we know which sector our stock is in, we can watch the sector index (or the futures contract based upon it — yes there are even futures contracts for sector indices!) which may give us even more confidence (or otherwise) in our potential trade. If the sector as a whole is strong, it is likely to carry our stock with it. If the index futures are a magnet, the sector futures are little fridge magnets; not hugely powerful, but they can be very useful.

Sector indices have another use. We can use *sector analysis* to find good trading candidates using a top down approach. For example, on a particular day we note that the market as a whole is moving strongly upwards. We look at the sector indices and find the strongest sector. We then look at the component stocks of that sector and find the strongest ones, which we then watch closely for possible long trades. We're trying to swim with the tide here, putting as much probability on our side as possible.

Naturally the sector indices can be charted themselves, and in the same way we watch the index futures charts, watching these sector charts can give us a slight edge by showing where our stock may go next.

Like the other market internals, the sector indices are nowhere near as important as the time and sales or the index futures. They are another tool to keep in our trading toolbox and use when the time is right, which might be when we need to find strongly trending sectors because we don't have enough stocks to watch, or when indecision reigns supreme and we need something extra to give us confidence in our trading decisions.

Chapter 15 - Putting It All Together

Now we have our watch list of stocks, some charts to put them on, more charts showing us what the futures are doing, and a time and sales screen, it's time to trade. We're going to put everything we've covered into practice, and walk through a trade. Let's go!

If trading the early part of the session, watch the first thirty minutes closely. Go through the watch list to see which stocks have gapped, and which are showing signs of making good opening range patterns, that is, those that are showing a clear bias towards the top or bottom of their early range.

If trading later in the day, have a look at what the stocks have done already, where the key support and resistance levels are, and if any stocks on the watch list have been trending or just going sideways. Look at the volume too. Not every stock that had news on it will end up moving strongly, some for whatever reason will just drift. We don't want to waste time on these, so if a stock is hardly trading any volume, strike it from the list early on so that you have more time to look at the ones which may be more worthwhile.

Try to find good potential long and short trade candidates so that you have options whichever way the market goes. Also keep an eye on the futures. Are they running away or just going sideways? All this time you are building an opinion of market sentiment.

After the first thirty minutes (or twenty minutes when you have at least six months experience), draw in the early range highs and lows on your charts to make it easy to spot good trading patterns forming.

Continue to scan through your charts looking at all of the above criteria. Many people make the mistake of trying to watch too many charts at the same time. They have lots of monitors hooked up to their PCs, all covered in charts. There's really no need for this, indeed it just makes life more difficult. Ideally you should have just three charts open at once:

1. The stock you are watching

2. The NASDAQ futures

3. The NYSE futures

If you are only trading NASDAQ stocks, then you can remove the NYSE futures chart.

In your stock chart window, bring up the first stock on your watch list. Ask yourself if there is good volume, if there is a bias of price to one side of the early range, if the stock is moving cleanly or is just chopping all over the place with no sense of direction. With the answers, you can make a decision as to whether it could be setting up into a potential trading pattern or not. If it isn't then move onto the next stock on your list, and repeat. When you've looked at the last stock on the list, go back to the first one and start over.

Keep cycling through the stocks in the same way. With practice, you will be able to look at a chart and decide in just a few seconds if it is setting up into a tradable pattern or not.

Once you have found a potential trade, keep that chart in front of you and watch for the entry to be confirmed. Are the futures going in the right direction (up if your potential trade is a long or down if it is a short)? If the pattern is an Early Range BreakOut or an Opening Reversal, then watch the time and sales closely. Are there more buys than sells? Bigger buys than bigger sells? How are traders reacting as the price approaches the breakout point? Does the tape accelerate or does it slow down? Remember, the tape tells you exactly what other traders are actually doing right now, it is your window on what is happening to this stock price.

Continuing your analysis, do the market internals confirm the direction that the futures are showing? Look at support and resistance levels. Is there anything that might stop the move once it's underway? Where will you get out if this trade goes against you? Where might you take profit? Is the potential reward worth the risk? Does this trade fit your money management plan? In other words, can you afford to lose whatever the maximum risk is and still remain within your money management criteria?

Trade Entry

If everything is in your favour, and the price itself confirms (on the time and sales screen in the case of momentum breakout trades), pull the trigger straight away. Do not hesitate, this is not the time to start doubting yourself or the strategy.

When entering, you should use a limit order if you can. Have your limit order ready to go on your trading platform, at the price you think the breakout is plus (or minus, for a short) a couple of cents.

The instant your entry order is filled, remember to put in a stop order so that in the case of something going wrong, you know what your maximum loss will be.

Then, most importantly, write down entry details for later analysis. Note the symbol for the stock, the price you entered, where you have placed your stop, the pattern the chart was making, and where you think you might exit.

Manage The Trade

Now you are in the trade you must manage it. Watch the price and see if it goes where you expected. If it doesn't, or the time and sales doesn't show follow up momentum in the few seconds following your entry (in the case of breakout patterns) how much room will you give it? How much time? If it's a breakout momentum type trade and it just goes sideways, the longer it does so the less chance of it ever following through, so get out quickly with as small a loss as possible, don't wait for your stop order to be hit. You can always enter again later if the price makes another breakout.

Keep an eye on the futures, and the advance / decline line. If they turn against you, be ready to exit. On the other hand if they are strongly in your favour (going up whilst you are in a long trade or down whilst you are short) you might give your trade more room or time.

Watch the time and sales for the early stages of the trade. Is the momentum still with you? If it has turned against you be ready to close out. Once you are in profit by 10-15 cents or so, the time and sales is no longer important. Momentum has got you into the trade with low risk, so the job of time and sales is done.

As soon as you are in profit by 10-15 cents, move your stop order to the entry price. Discounting slippage and commissions, the worst that can happen now is you will exit at break even. Your trade has just become risk-free!

Now watch for your target. If something happens to suggest the move is over before it gets hit, consider exiting the trade, or at least using a comfort exit and getting out half of your position. On the other hand if it blasts through your target and keeps going, think about where your new target should be.

Watch your stop order. Has the price moved enough into profit to consider moving it again to lock in some profit should it get hit?

Last but not least, remember to breathe! It seems like there is a lot to do, but with practice it will become very easy.

After The Trade

Once out of the trade, write down the exit details (see Log and Analyse in the next chapter) and then be ready for the next one. If you took a loss, so what? That is part of the business of trading and is to be expected. As long as you executed the trade properly, that's all that matters.

Whatever you do, don't let a losing trade get you down, keep a clear head. Concentrate on the next trade, but don't revenge trade to try and get your money back, you will only end up losing more.

Remember also that the trade you just exited might have further to go. Perhaps the reason you got out turned out to be just a minor wiggle. Perhaps the breakout didn't work, but now it is set to break out again and this time has more momentum. Always be prepared to enter the same stock again.

If you are trading the later part of the day, have a look at the FinViz HeatMaps and Yahoo's Most Active lists, and any other scanners you may have access to, to find out what stocks have been moving well and therefore might present more trading opportunities. Stocks that put in stellar moves in the morning often make great moves in the afternoon as they retrace some of their earlier gains or losses, so in this case scanners (including the free ones mentioned) can be a useful tool.

CHAPTER 16 - LOG & ANALYSE

In the previous chapter a couple of references were made to writing down trade details as you enter and exit your trades. Keeping accurate records in this way is crucial, for several reasons.

The most important of these is to be able to find out where your losses are coming from. Some losses are to be expected, not every pattern will work out according to plan. However by going back and looking at losing trades after the market has closed and you are completely emotionally detached, you will be able to easily see if a losing trade was down to something you did wrong (such as entering before confirmation, going against the futures, or taking a long just below a major resistance level), or because the pattern simply didn't work this time. And if the pattern didn't work, you will also be able to see if you took your loss at a sensible place, or if you left it to run on too far in the hope that it would turn into a win.

Winning trades should also be analysed. If you find that one particular pattern is accounting for all your profits, you may want to consider dropping the other setups and concentrating all your efforts on this pattern. You'll also want to see if you extracted as much profit from your winning trades as there was on offer.

There are other more subtle things you may notice from your analysis, such as finding that certain stocks perform better than others, or that different times of the day are more profitable for you.

What To Log

The more information you can record about each trade, the better. However, you don't want to spend more time writing down your trades than you spend watching the market, so here are some essentials to note:

- The stock you are trading
- The time you entered
- The number of shares you entered with
- The pattern that signalled the entry along with any other factors that contributed to it (futures, time and sales, etc).

If you have time, you should also try and record how you were feeling at the time you took the trade. You will learn a lot from this!

When the trade is complete, you need to note down:

- The time you exited the trade

- What made you decide to exit

- How you rated your execution of the trade at the time. When scoring yourself you can use a scale of 1-5 with 1 being very bad, and 5 being perfect execution.

Finally, at the end of each day you should also total up the number of winning trades and the number of losing trades, the size of the average win, and the size of the average loss. Keep an eye on these numbers over time, remembering that the aim is for the average win to far exceed the average loss. In this way you can have more losing trades than winning ones and still make money overall.

After The Market Closes

Writing all these things down will help whether you read them back or not, but to get the maximum benefit of your trade logging, you really should analyse what you have written.

The earliest you should do this is after the market has closed. The best time though, is at the weekend, when the markets are closed and you have had time to become properly detached from your earlier trading actions.

Go through your notes and if you can, bring up a chart for each stock you traded. From your clear-headed weekend perspective, examine the chart and see if you would still trade it the way you did on the day. If the trade was a winner, ask yourself if you could have done anything to make it a bigger winner. Could you have entered a bit sooner? Exited later? If the trade was a loser, again, ask yourself if you could have done anything better.

Be brutally honest with yourself throughout this process. It can be difficult at first, but like anything, it will become easier with time. It really is the best way to improve your performance.

Chapter 17 - Golden Rules

Here are my golden rules of trading. Stick to these and you'll have a much better chance of success.

1. Never let a winning trade turn into a losing one. Ever! If the price turns around, it's better to get out with a small profit or at break even than wait for the trade to end up as a loss.

2. You don't have to trade. If there are no really good trades on offer, don't just trade for the sake of it. Look for quality trades, not quantity. Deciding not to enter a trade is just as valid and important a decision as taking a trade.

3. Don't think about money, only think in terms of points. It will make the losses easier to handle, and it will also make it easier to increase your size with experience.

4. Never get emotional about the market. Remember you have no control over it, getting angry wont make it go your way. Concentrate on your execution because that is something you can control. Get the execution right and the profits will take care of themselves. Use the methods in the Chapter Twelve to help with this.

5. Trade with as many factors going your way as possible. If the market is going up, and the sector, and the futures, why take a short? The more things in your favour, the greater the probability the trade will work out.

6. Stay away from choppy charts with no direction. Look for something better. If there is nothing better, don't trade.

7. If you find you are *hoping* or *wishing* that the price will go up or down, then there is something wrong with this trade and you should probably be getting out of it.

8. Think like a trader. Look for things other traders will be looking for, don't try and be clever. If a trade doesn't jump out at you from a chart, it's probably not there. If you can't see it, who else will?

9. Record all of your trades and analyse them after the trading session (ideally at the weekend) when you are emotionally detached from the market and can look back objectively. Learn from every trade, winners and losers alike.

10. Always remain flexible and open to what the market is telling you. You could be in a perfectly set up trade with everything going your way, but if the market suddenly decides to run the other way, get out fast and ask questions later.

11. Maintain a distraction-free environment. Trading requires concentration. The charts only need your undivided attention for a few hours a day, so switch off the iPod and the mobile phone, close the door, and hang out the "do not disturb" sign. The distractions will still be there for you when you're done.

12. Prepare mentally. Think like a winner. Know that you can succeed! It is a cliché I know, but trading is mentally tough and it can be all too easy to become downhearted after a few losing trades.

13. Don't try and catch every available trade every day, it's just not possible. If you're busy managing a trade, then it is quite likely you'll miss another one. That's part of the business, we can't catch them all.

14. Be professional. Just because you can start trading without a college degree and years of training, doesn't mean this job is easier or less demanding than any other. Take it seriously, put in the effort, and you will reap the rewards. If you treat it as a joke, or decide to simply "have a go and see what happens", you'll not get far.

When you are ready to trade, start by paper trading (simulated trading). Go through all the steps as if you were going to trade for real, but instead of actually entering a trade through your broker software, instead note down the price at which you would have done so. Manage the trade exactly as you would if it were real, and then note your exit price. Don't cheat when you do this, and scribble out the losers or change your mind about where you would have entered, you're only cheating yourself.

If you can, use a trading simulator to paper trade with, it will make the experience more realistic and the transition to live trading easier. Simulators are designed to look like real trading software, but instead of transmitting your order to the market, they just keep track of it internally. They give you that live trading experience, but with none of the risk. There are lots of simulators around, a web search should find plenty to choose from.

I know many traders believe that simulated trading is a waste of time, but I couldn't disagree with them more. Simulation is one of the greatest tools available to the novice trader, and to experienced traders too when learning new strategies. It gives you the opportunity to learn the ropes, and to make all your inevitable rookie mistakes with absolutely zero risk to your capital (if not to your ego!)

Trainee airline pilots use simulators for similar reasons. Aircraft are expensive, so it's better to crash a virtual one when learning to land. No airline would risk letting a pilot loose on a real aircraft without some simulator time, and no trader should risk their money in the market without the same.

The main argument levelled at simulated trading is that it doesn't present the same psychological challenge to the trader as using real money. This is certainly true. However, why put money at risk while learning the basics? If you can't trade profitably on a simulator when there's much less psychological pressure, it is clear you won't be able to do so in the real market where the pressure is equally real. Far better to find out your limitations and weaknesses in the sim, and then work on improving there, where the cost is nil.

Going Live

Once you are at the stage where you are making regular profits in your paper or simulated trading, it is time to switch to live trading. Start trading very small sizes, just 100 shares at a time. At this size, every 1 cent move in the stock price will be worth $1 profit or loss to your account. Even with this very limited risk, you will be amazed how much more difficult it seems now that cash is on the line. Remember to think in terms of points not money.

When you are consistently profitable, for example when you have reached an overall profit of $1000 trading only 100 shares at a time, or when you are profitable four days our of every five, move up to trading 200 shares at a time. If you are thinking in terms of points not cash then this move will be easier.

Once again, stick with this size until you are consistently profitable before stepping it up to trading 300 shares a go. If you continue to build up your trading size in this manner, 100 shares at a time, you won't get wiped out by a big losing day, and they will happen no matter how well you are trading.

Should you experience a run of losses, cut your trade size in half. This is the opposite of what you will want to do, because you'll be wanting to win back the money you've lost. It will take longer to recover your losses when trading smaller size, but everyone hits a bad run once on a while, and you need to minimise the damage and the risk, especially at these times when the psychological pressure is at its greatest.

If you still keep losing, go back to paper or a simulator for a while to regain your form and your confidence, and then build up from there again.

Never be tempted to take short cuts and trade bigger size in order to quickly make up your losses, this is a sure way to lose even more money very quickly indeed.

Part Four - Strategy Exercises

Introduction

The exercises on the following pages will give you an opportunity to practice recognising the chart patterns covered in Part Three of this book. After each chart segment and question set, the chart is repeated with some analysis added to it and an explanation of the patterns.

Unlike the exercises in Part Two, many of the charts here are shown before the pattern has completed. This is to help you in recognising patterns as they unfold on live charts. In each such exercise, an additional chart is also supplied with an explanation of how the pattern developed.

Where horizontal lines are already drawn in, these represent the previous day's high, low, and close prices. The vertical line on each chart signifies the start of the trading session.

Exercise 1 Questions

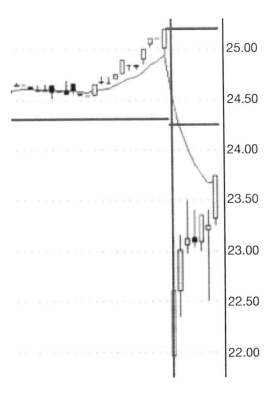

1. What pattern is this?

2. Where is the entry?

3. Where is a good potential exit (or exits)?

4. Where would you exit if the trade failed?

Exercise 1 Answers

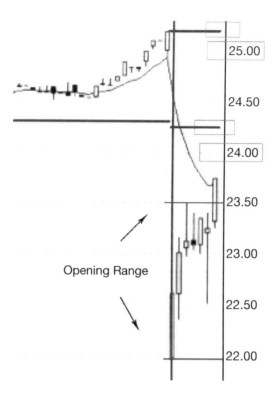

1. By drawing in the early range lines we can easily see that this pattern is an early range breakout. The fact that the price had consolidated just above a whole number before breaking out gives this trade added probability of success.

2. The entry is when the price breaks above the early range high at $23.50.

3. The first potential exit is the whole number of $24, then there is another at the previous day's low, and the third potential exit area is the whole number of $25 and then previous day's close at $25.20. These are marked here with the boxes.

4. If the trade did not follow through quickly, then we would exit no lower than $23.40.

Exercise 1 Result

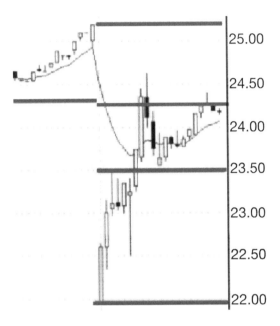

We see that the price broke straight through the whole number at $24, then went through the previous day's low, but fell back down again.

A suitable exit strategy as this chart unfolded would have been to have closed half the position at the previous day's low ($24.25), then the other half when the price fell back below the whole number of $24, so perhaps close out at $23.90.

Trading 1000 shares would have yielded the following:

- Buy 1000 @ $23.55
- Sell 500 @ $24.25 = 70 cents per share = $350
- Sell 500 @ $23.95 = 40 cents per share = $200
- Total profit = $550

One final point to note on this chart is that when the price fell back down, it bounced off the breakout point (the early high at $23.50) and went back up again. A classic example of previous resistance becoming new support.

Exercise 2 Questions

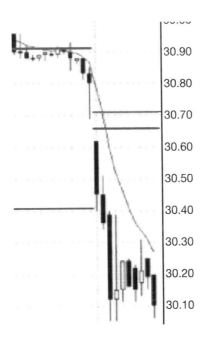

1. What pattern is this?

2. Where might you take an entry?

3. What would be a good exit (or exits)?

4. Where would you get out if it failed?

5. Is there anything to be cautious about?

Exercise 2 Answers

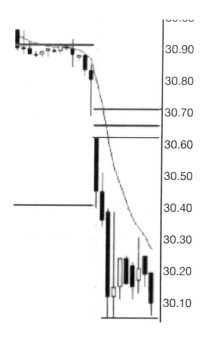

1. Again, the first thing to do is draw in the early range high and low lines. We can see that the price is setting up to make an early range breakout to the downside. All of the price so far has been contained within the 10 EMA, adding to the probability of success for the trade.

2. The entry will be just below the early range low, i.e. just below the lower line.

3. The price is already below the previous day's high and low, so we cannot use those as exits. Instead, we need to use whole numbers, the 3-bar rule, and the 10 EMA. Because the 10 EMA has already been containing the price, it seems logical that we should use that to tell us when to exit here.

4. If the trade failed we would want to get out as soon as it came back above the lower line, in other words as soon as it came back within the early range. Thus our initial stop order could be at $30.10

5. There is a major reason for caution on this chart, and that is that we are just above a decade number, $30. Ideally then, our entry should be below not only the lower line, but also just below the decade number.

Exercise 2 Result

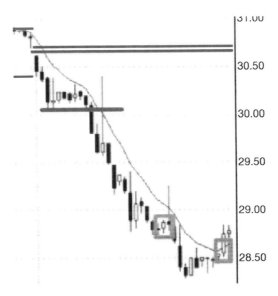

Looking at how this chart panned out, we can see that the price broke down through the early range low and the decade number. It fell heavily, stalling briefly at the whole number of $29 on its way.

The first box shows the price spiking through the EMA. Although it is not possible to tell from the chart alone, this was caused by a single trade going off well outside the bid/ask spread, and was not a cause for concern.

As the 10 EMA was containing the price so well, it would have made sense to wait for the price to break through it to signal our exit. This finally happened at around $28.60, also highlighted on the chart.

Trading 1000 shares would have yielded the following:

- Sell (Short) 1000 at $29.90 - allowing it to break through the decade number
- Buy (Cover) 1000 at $28.60 = $1.30 per share = $1300
- Total profit before brokerage commission = $1300

Exercise 3 Questions

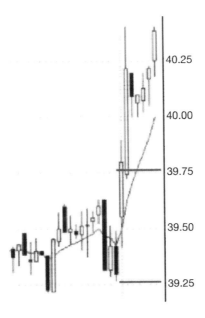

1. What pattern is this?

2. Where might you take an entry?

3. What would be a good exit (or exits)?

4. Where would you get out if it failed?

Exercise 3 Answers

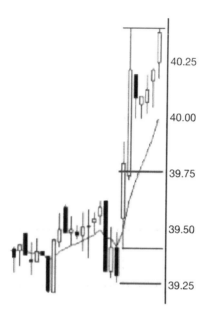

1. Drawing in the high and low (the thicker lines here) makes it easy to see that the chart is setting up for a potential early range breakout above the high, so we would be looking to go long (buy). The price is showing bias to the upside, and is contained within the 10 EMA. Also note that it has already exceeded the previous day's high, suggesting this stock is strong indeed.

2. Entry would be when the price breaks above the high, so around $40.42.

3. As the price has already gone past the previous day's high, we couldn't use that as an exit, so we would use the next round number ($41), and also consider using the EMA as it has contained the price action nicely so far.

4. If the breakout failed we would, as usual, want to exit as soon as possible. If the price went back down we would want to exit no later than about $40.30.

Exercise 3 Result

The price did break out to the upside, and kept going until it got to the whole number. It went through that number, but came back down and closed below it. If you think back to the section on bars in Part One of this book, you will remember that a bar such as that highlighted in the middle of the box can signal a change of direction when taken in context. So an ideal exit would be the whole number $41.

If we missed that one, then the break of the EMA shown in the second box would have been a good time to exit.

If we entered at $40.42 as planned, we would have realised a profit of 58 cents per share, which is $580 when trading 1000 shares.

Finally on this chart, notice how once again the assumed resistance line that was drawn at the early range high, later becomes support when the price moves back down.

Exercise 4 Questions

1. What pattern is this?

2. Where might you take an entry?

3. What would be a good exit (or exits)?

4. Where would you get out if it failed?

Exercise 4 Answers

1. The chart is setting up for an early range breakout to the downside (price is showing bias towards the low). The price has also remained below the 10 EMA for almost the whole session so far.

2. Entry would be taken on a break of the low, so around $40.45 here.

3. With the decade number of $40 below, that would make an ideal exit for all or half the position. We could of course, use the 10 EMA as well.

4. If the price came back inside the early range we would know that the breakout had failed. We would want to exit no later than $40.55 for a maximum loss of 10 cents per share.

Exercise 4 Result

The price broke out below the low. It blasted through the decade number at $40 and then bounced briefly off the next whole number at $39. This would have been a sensible place to close half the trade (a comfort exit).

The price continued down and went through the next whole number of $38. However, the next candlestick is very bullish. It reversed all of the move made by the previous candle in one go. As it made such a dramatic up-move, and also broke back up through a whole number, this would have been a good place to exit the rest of our position. Alternatively, we could have held on for a break back through the 10 EMA.

Assuming we took the first two exits signalled, the profit trading 1000 shares would have worked out like this:

- Sell (Short) 1000 shares at $40.45
- Buy (Cover) 500 shares at $39 = $1.45 per share = $725
- Buy (Cover) 500 shares at $38 = $2.45 per share = $1225
- Total profit before broker commission = $1950

Exercise 5 Questions

1. What pattern is this?

2. Where might you take an entry?

3. What would be a good exit (or exits)?

4. Where would you get out if it failed?

5. What is there on this chart that would make you cautious?

Exercise 5 Answers

1. The price opened below the close of the previous day, so this share has gapped down. We can see that the price went up but failed to close the gap. In other words it didn't get back up to the previous day's closing price. Instead it turned around and came back down to the opening price shown by the horizontal (red) line and broke through it. Thus the pattern is an Opening Reversal.

2. The entry was when the stock broke through down the opening price, which we can see here was about $29.95.

3. We could use whole numbers, the 10 EMA, or the 3-bar rule to exit.

4. The pattern would be considered to have failed if the price rose back above the opening price (lower thick line). As we have a whole number ($23) just above, we could place our stop just above that at around $25.03 because we know that whole numbers can act as resistance.

5. The previous day's low is marked on the chart just below where we are considering an entry. Therefore we might want to wait and see if the price breaks below this before taking the short trade.

Exercise 5 Result

The price broke down through the previous day's low, it never came back anywhere near our stop loss order. The best exit was when the price broke through the 10 EMA.

Depending on how aggressively or conservatively we were trading, we could have exited either on the candle that briefly broke through the EMA, or waited until two candles later when the candle actually closed above the EMA. In this trade it wouldn't have made much difference either way. As the EMA had gone flat anyway, the earlier exit would have been preferable.

Assuming we waited for the break of the previous day's low and entered our short position at a price of $22.85, we would have had the following result:

- Sell (Short) 1000 shares at $22.85
- Buy (Cover) 1000 shares at $22.65 = 20 cents per share = $200
- Total before commission = $200

Not quite as profitable as the previous example, but the important thing is that the trade is managed correctly.

Exercise 6 Questions

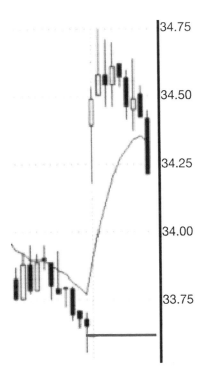

1. What pattern is this?

2. Where might you take an entry?

3. What would be a good exit (or exits)?

4. Where would you get out if it failed?

Exercise 6 Answers

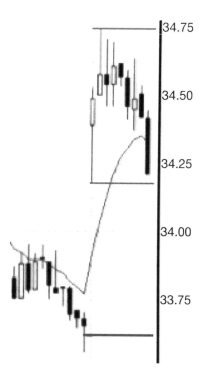

1. The early range high and low prices have been marked with the thicker lines. The price gapped from the previous day's close. It carried on going up, but then turned around and started descending. If the price then breaks out below the early range low, then this pattern will be an Opening Reversal and we would be looking to sell (go short).

2. Entry would be taken once the price broke through the lower line — the early range low. So roughly $34.18

3. In an Opening Reversal of this type we are ideally anticipating the price closing the gap — i.e. going back to yesterday's close price, which is $33.62. We would of course be cautious at the round number of $34 and may consider closing half the position if the price stalls there.

4. The pattern would be considered failed if the price came back into the early range, so as usual we would want our stop price to be just above that, around $34.25 seems reasonable.

Exercise 6 Result

The price did indeed break down below the early range low, so we would have gone short. However, in this case the pattern failed and the price quickly came back up.

Our stop was at $34.25, so on this trade we would have taken a loss of 7 cents per share, which on 1000 shares is $70. Every winning trade shown so far has made well in excess of $70 profit, so we can see the importance of keeping our losses as small as possible. After the previous trades, this is not going to make a very big dent in our account.

Later on in the trading session, notice that the price then broke out through the early range high resistance line we drew in right at the start of the day, after having made an ascending triangle pattern. If we traded this and exited at the whole number of $35 (which coincided nicely with the previous day's high and thus was strong resistance), this would have given us a profit of about 20 cents per share. On 1000 shares, that's $200. So even after our previous loss, this share could still have made us a net profit of $130 on this particular day.

Exercise 7 Questions

1. What pattern is this?

2. Where might you take an entry?

3. What would be a good exit (or exits)?

4. Where would you get out if it failed?

5. Are there any reasons to be cautious or delay entry?

Exercise 7 Answers

1. The pattern is an early range breakout. There is little bias here, but the price has already started to break below the early range low.

2. See the answer to question 5.

3. A whole number exit could be used, or as the price is now below the 10 EMA we could also use that. Of course there is the 3-bar exit rule as well.

4. A stop order just inside the early range, would take us out of the trade if the pattern failed, so around $37.65

5. We have the previous day's closing price and low price just below, and as we know these may act as support we may want to delay our entry until the price broke down through them.

Exercise 7 Result

The price fell down below all of the support lines we had drawn in, so we could have made a short entry around $37.50.

The first rule-based exit occurs when the price breaks back through the EMA. This also occurs around at the same time the price breaks back above the whole number of $37, which means it is showing strength.

Exiting there would have made us around 45 cents per share, which is $450 when trading 1000 shares.

An alternative exit for at least half the position is the doji candle immediately followed by an up candle (in the oval area). If you remember back to Part One, the doji represents indecision, and the up candle immediately following it is a strong signal of a change of direction.

Exercise 8 Questions

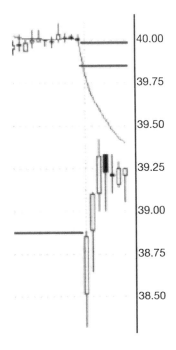

1. What pattern is this?

2. Where might you take an entry?

3. What would be a good exit (or exits)?

4. Where would you get out if it failed?

Exercise 8 Answers

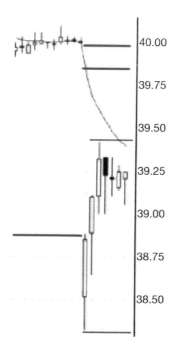

1. Although the price has gapped down, it is not showing any sign of reversing direction. Instead it looks like it may well break out above the early range high. So this is an Early Range BreakOut in the making.

2. Entry would be on the break of the high, so around $39.42.

3. Ideally we would be looking for the price to close the gap, that is, to return to the closing price of the previous day which we can see is $39.98. That's only 2 cents away from the decade number $40 as well, so this seems a sensible target. However, we would be cautious around $39.85 which is the previous day's low, knowing that this level may provide resistance.

4. We would know the pattern had failed if the price came back within the early range, and so would want to exit no later than $39.35 for a maximum loss of 7 cents per share.

Exercise 8 Result

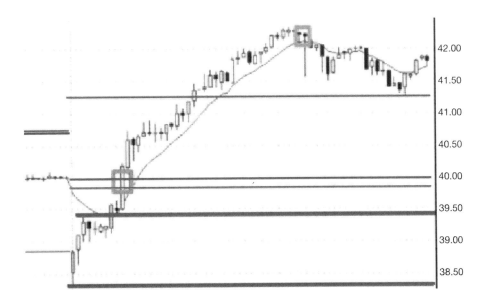

The price broke out and flew straight through our target area of $40. It carried on right through the previous day's high ($41.25) and kept on going. The 10 EMA followed it cleanly all the way, so we could have used that to exit all or part of the position.

If we traded 1000 shares, and assume we closed half the position at the original target regardless, and the other half when the EMA failed, we would have made the following:

- Buy 1000 at $39.42
- Sell 500 at $40.00 = 58 cents per share = $290
- Sell 500 at $42.00 = $2.58 per share = $1290
- Total profit before commission = $1580

Finally, notice how the previous day's high at $41.25 became support later in the day when the price bounced off it towards the end of the chart.

Exercise 9 Questions

1. What late session entry can you see on this chart (that is, an entry pattern that occurred in the latter half of the trading session)?

2. What was a good exit (or exits)?

3. Where would your stop have been if the trade turned against you?

Exercise 9 Answers

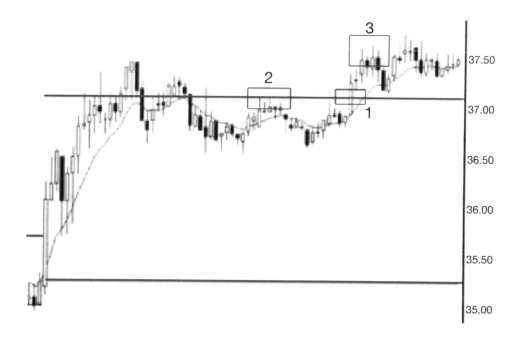

1. The entry was signalled by the price breaking through the previous day's high (box 1). That previous high ($37.09) had already proved itself as resistance when the price bounced off it earlier in the session, highlighted by box 2, thus making this breakout more significant.

2. The exit on this chart was a little more difficult. Waiting for a break of the 10 EMA would have yielded little profit. However the EMA had not been cleanly containing the price throughout the day, that is to say, because the price had been crossing up and down over the EMA all day, it had little significance for this stock on this particular session and therefore was not going to be a good exit indicator for this trade. A better exit would have been to read the price candles (or bars), and see that the price started going sideways around the $37.50 area (box 3). As moves later in the session tend to be smaller and slower, such sideways action at this time of the day would be a good enough reason to exit with about 40 cents per share profit. The important point to understand here is that there is rarely a right or wrong time to exit a trade, as traders we must make use of all the information available to us and make a decision based on what the chart is showing us, and our own experience built up over time.

3. If the price fell back below the previous day's high then the trade would have failed. A good place for a stop order would be just below the whole number of $37 as we know this is likely to provide support. So around $36.95 would be a sensible place.

Finally, note there was also an early range breakout with a good target of a whole number and previous day's high also signalled at the start of this chart.

Exercise 10 Questions

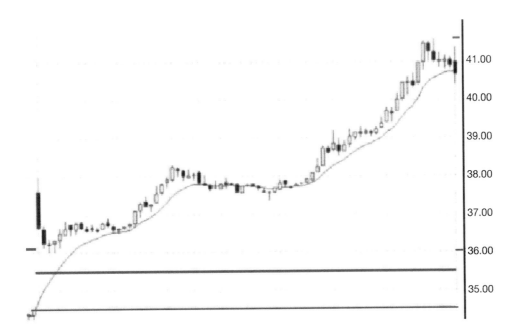

1. Can you see any entry patterns in the later part of this chart?

2. What was a good exit (or exits)?

3. Where would your stop have been if the trade turned against you?

Exercise 10 Answers

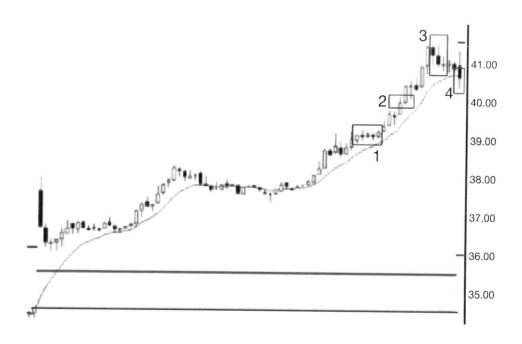

1. There is a 1234 consolidation pattern highlighted in the box number 1. The price consolidated in four relatively small range bars just above a whole number ($39), and at the time this was the high of the day. The entry was when the price went above the high of the fourth bar of the pattern, which was around $39.25.

2. The first exit was the decade number of $40 (box 2), giving 75 cents per share profit (=$750 on 1000 shares). If we held on to half the position, then the next signalled exit was when we saw three bars against us (box 3). Had we held on past that, we would have needed to close out the position at the end of the day at around $40.67 (box 4, also a break of the EMA.) Remember as day traders we never hold overnight, we don't want to be exposed to risks such as news items outside of trading hours.

3. We could have placed our initial stop just below the 10 EMA which, by the time of the pattern, was following the price cleanly. This was also just below the whole number of $39 which we know would provide support. So $38.95 would be a good area.

Exercise 11 Questions

1. What can you see on this chart that might make you take a late session entry?

2. Where would you have entered?

3. What was a good exit (or exits)?

4. Where would your stop have been if the trade turned against you?

Exercise 11 Answers

1. For much of the session the price has been bouncing off $93.50, so this has become resist-ance. In the area shown by box 1, we see that the price has been consolidating just below this resistance line, suggesting it might break above it soon. If the price breaks through that level, we have a good long entry.

2. The entry was when the price broke above the resistance, so around $93.55.

3. The whole number (box 2) made a good exit at $94 giving a quick profit of 45 cents per share (=$450 when trading 1000 shares). Holding on to half the position and using the 10 EMA to exit the rest would have yielded around 95 cents per share on the remainder.

4. We know that resistance once broken, often becomes support. So if the price broke above the $93.50 resistance then broke back down below it, we would know the trade was not work-ing. Thus a good place for an initial stop would be $93.45, which would mean a maximum loss of 10 cents a share. Knowing we had a whole number target of 45 cents, we would see that the risk : reward on this trade was 1:4.5.

LEARN FOREX TRADING

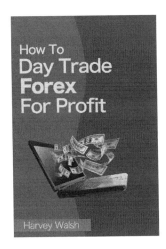

Expand your trading skills and learn to trade the multi-trillion dollar foreign exchange market. Written in his trademark plain English chatty style, Harvey Walsh's latest book teaches you everything you need to know to start trading forex. It covers everything from understanding how currencies work and what makes them move, to how to open your first forex broker account and place your first trades.

The book also includes detailed trading setups for the forex market, as well as advice on how to create your own, giving you more of an edge.

How To Day Trade Forex For Profit is available now from all good book stores.

Made in the USA
Middletown, DE
22 January 2015